A FIRE RUNS
THROUGH ALL THINGS

A FIRE
RUNS
THROUGH
ALL THINGS

SUSAN MURPHY

ZEN KOANS
FOR FACING
THE CLIMATE
CRISIS

SHAMBHALA

Shambhala Publications, Inc.
2129 13th Street
Boulder, Colorado 80302
www.shambhala.com

The haiku that appear at the end of each chapter are from *Cloud Hands*
by Ron Moss (Launceston, Tasmania: Walleah Press, 2021).
Reprinted by arrangement with the author.

Cover art: Kasamatsu Shirō, *Shadow of a Mountain*, 1959, color woodblock print.
Clark Art Institute, gift of the Rodbell Family Collection, 2014.16.48
Cover design: Daniel Urban-Brown
Interior design: Daniel Urban-Brown

9 8 7 6 5 4 3 2 1

First Edition
Printed in the United States of America

Shambhala Publications makes every effort to print on acid-free, recycled paper.
Shambhala Publications is distributed worldwide by Penguin Random House,
Inc., and its subsidiaries.

Library of Congress Cataloging-in-Publication Data
Names: Murphy, Susan, 1950– author.
Title: A fire runs through all things: Zen koans for facing the climate crisis /
Susan Murphy.
Description: Boulder: Shambhala, 2023.
Identifiers: LCCN 2023005647 | ISBN 9781645471080 (trade paperback)
Subjects: LCSH: Koan. | Climatic changes—Religious aspects—Buddhism. |
Environmental protection—Religious aspects—Buddhism.
Classification: LCC BQ9289.5 .M876 2023 | DDC 294.3/443—dc23/
eng/20230213
LC record available at https://lccn.loc.gov/2023005647

In loving memory of Uncle Max (Dulumunmun) Harrison,
Yuin Elder

And for Jack and Maeve,
my grandchildren, Maya, Thomas, and Elio,
and all the generations down from here:
may the brave constancy of your lives help
transform a crazed world

CONTENTS

PREFACE

My path to this book and a life marked by Zen winds from a barefoot early childhood spent in the warm Australian tropics of Far North Queensland. There, until the age of eight, I spent my time exploring ancient rainforests said to have originated in another age, in the southern supercontinent of Gondwanaland, and floating, goggle-eyed, over the Great Barrier Reef. I came of age in a shabby part of inner-city Sydney that was just on the cusp of losing its slum status and becoming sought after by artists and thinkers. In loving the many stimulations of that beautiful harbor city, however, I never lost the elemental impressions of my early childhood, to the point where I often walked barefoot on city pavements because all things and people were more alive and present to me that way.

The strong draw of the natural world never receded in me. Trees continued to confirm what was true and unimpeachable. Cats perched primly on walls in meditation. Scattering seagulls loudly exclaimed the wide give of beaches. Clouds freely accepted close watching from the rooftop of our house, where I repaired to read books, my back against the sun-warmed chimney. And the sound of rain on a tin roof continued to create the most intimate refuge of all possible being. You cannot take the early childhood experience of being seamless with the flowing natural world out of a human being. For me it set a course of fierce, protective love of this Earth. "Become like this" and "I'm all yours" still feel like the innermost words of the natural world addressed to my soul.

And it was so in my older brother and sister, too. One night when I was twelve, the three of us sat together long after dinner had ended, talking our way deep into the unnerving civilizational suicide wish detectible in our world, one that appears shockingly indifferent to the collateral damage it heaps upon the natural world. Our species was already openly contemplating the possibility of extinction by its own hand from a number of possible causes, all of them officially considered "sane." Between mutually assured nuclear destruction and the threat posed by humanity's war on the environment, we could already feel our civilization almost zealously embracing apocalypse in the form of unstoppable growth, unceasing "progress," and our undying self-regard as the dominant species.

Perhaps children are always more sensitive to the glaringly obvious than adults can afford to be. But it is a deeply informative moment when a child detects a seemingly unmentionable death wish in the adults of their own society. Around the kitchen table that night we consciously chose to look at the industrial-strength assault of an exploding human population on a shrinking and collapsing natural world. Our family was far from wealthy, but we felt the shame of the deepening cycles of exploitation, injustice, poverty, and hunger that the "underdeveloped" world was apparently expected to bear on behalf of our own relatively comfortable lives.

That we might be the last generation to live on a planet with live coral reefs, seas full of fish, tigers roaming free, and a vast and intact Amazon rainforest felt unthinkable, even intolerable—yet the possibility had to be admitted. Caught up in an unstoppable rush of facts and feelings until the wee hours of the morning, in a state of terror curiously mixed with something intensely alive in us, we three weighed the fate of the world and stared directly at our own complicity in that fate.

It hardly needs saying that directly facing this terror and waking up together in this way was made possible by our love for one another. When we finally called it a night around three in the morning, I felt flattened, crushed—but also enlarged with the thrilling sense of having taken on a little of the mantle of painful adult awareness that is the true weight of the world.

I remember the next morning as very bright—even too bright after the latest late night of my life to that point. I heaped cereal into my bowl, and milk, then walked to the same high-backed chair of the night before. That extraordinary night lay inside me like a kaleidoscope of amazing pieces of knowledge, shards of feeling sharp to the touch, overwhelmingly complicated and strangely precious. I set my bowl on the table. I took hold of the back of the chair and pulled it out. I sat down and put my hands on the table.

And exactly then, from nowhere, came a tidal wave of marvelous awareness that swept me up beyond all reach of doubt that all is well and completely at ease. This assurance was somehow utterly undisturbed by the equally plain fact that we chanced to be alive in a moment of slow-burning catastrophe, not just for ourselves, our family, or our nation, but for the entire life system of the planet. "All things are well" is how the fifteenth-century English mystic and anchoress Juliana of Norwich put the same realization, "and all manner of things shall be well." The clear knowing of this rang through my bones and seemed vibrantly alive right inside every terrifying complication of the rejoinder "and so much is wrong."

I was astonished, and yet it seemed the astonishment of remembering some tremendous thing I'd always known but strangely forgotten, something very deep-lying and fundamentally fearless, even in the face of my overwhelming concern.

In fact, it was intrinsic to such passionately aroused concern—stirred into life by it. And though I could not possibly say how, I knew that I moved step-by-step and hand in hand with it.

Everything—the chair and the kitchen table and the sitting down and the placing of my hands around my willow-patterned bowl of cereal—*everything* bestowed the inexplicable blessing: that we must rely exactly on what is happening to contain all we need, that we can dare to meet it fully, just as it is, and that what is so urgently being called up in us flows naturally and purely from an unqualified "yes" to a hard and even tragic reality.

And with it, an inarguable sense of reassurance that we are each not helpless at all, that we all actively make this mysterious and wondrous world together, and that everything that is here, everything we do, counts.

In trying to convey the astonishing immediacy of this piercing moment of recognition in an earlier work, *Minding the Earth, Mending the World*, in 2012, I reached for what Emily Dickinson is often quoted as saying: "Life is so startling, it leaves very little time for anything else."[1]

I was bruised by an equal wonder. A course was set. Don't miss anything. Everyone here counts. Find out what this means, and do what it wants of you.

In time, it was Zen practice and koan mind that ushered me into the reality that is so startling it makes infinite room for everything else. And it was Zen koan training that forensically examined how easily we can become so immune to our own locked-in dream state as human beings that we don't even realize we can wake up.

My Zen life began early in my thirties. I was writing a feature film I would later direct about the threat of mutually assured nuclear destruction and its dark logic, a logic that seems now to have worked insidiously to normalize the slower-motion planetary disaster of our climate crisis. The film, *Breathing Under Water*, attempted to plumb the underworld of the collective mind we all share in, a mind that could create a world so casually placed on the razor's edge. I needed to find a way to resolve in my own mind our hell-bent—yet almost casual—preparedness to place every living being and every rock and twig and cloud in jeopardy, each thing so powerfully here in its own right. That need was very alive in me the day I first stepped into a zendo for a weekend of practice. So was the need to reconcile the intimate quality of all things with the estranging power of my own mind. The radical, re-righting shift that I sensed was so alive in the mind of Zen drew me through that door.

In a small, rather dusty, candlelit garage in Sydney, repurposed for the weekend as an interview space, John Tarrant, director of the Pacific Zen Institute in Santa Rosa, California, sat waiting to offer me the jeopardy I was about to request. I recklessly asked for a koan and received "Mu," the usual first barrier to be met on the koan path. Of course, the only barrier is yourself. Mu lets you encounter the obdurate strength of this fact beyond a shadow of a doubt. Here it is:

A monk asks Zhaozhou, "Does a dog have buddhanature, or not?"

Zhaozhou replies, "Mu."

Mu, which variously gestures toward "not," "is not," "does not have," "does not not have," and "no-thing," is taken up in chapter 2. But for now, let's recognize *Mu* as simply being one syllable short of original silence opening far beyond yourself as the free-flowing, brimming emptiness of all things, undoing *monk, dog, buddha nature, have, have not* . . . When Mu has finished undoing *you* and *me*, as well, all things can rejoice in their original nature.

What impelled me at that moment was the deep intimation

from childhood that the clearest, living water of complete reality ran somewhere in me, and that I had to find my way to that stream, to drink from it and know it for my adult self.

Now I'd probably turn that around and say "be known by it" as myself.

Mu was the start of all the trouble, but trouble strictly of the best kind. Mu is one insult after another to the crowding, knowing mind. What Mu opens up and continues to affirm is the sense of wonder and curiosity called *not-knowing*. Mu makes room for the lived immensity of every moment, the refuge offered in every formless circumstance, however unlikely looking. Beyond even the reach of gratitude, Mu brings you home to where all the many beings, utterly distinct, are also not other than oneself.

That koan path wove through a decade of walking closely with a teacher through many hundreds of koans in dozens of *sesshins*, or seven-day silent Zen retreats, woven through a life thick with children and family, academic and creative work, a slowly collapsing marriage, a new but never easy love, and the piercing loss of my dearly beloved sister—all under the entire "hazy moon of enlightenment," to quote Keizan's lovely verse to Case 6, *Tranmissions of the Light*. Koans don't just sit alongside the griefs, joys, and disasters of life; they run to meet them and turn all suppositions mercifully inside out. They have sweet fit with the crises of life, resolving all things back (if you notice) to the undivided reality in which, despite our best human efforts, all life is actually taking place. I am indebted to the lot of it.

I am indebted, too, to a handful of Chinese Tang dynasty Zen masters for whose thorough entanglement with this book I make no apology, especially Zhaozhou Congshen (778–897), whom you will meet frequently throughout this book. But you will also have the lovely shock of encounters with other Zen masters: Mazu, Yunmen, Fayan, Xuedou, and Hongzhi in the Tang and Song dynasties in China; and Dogen, Keizan, Ikkyu, and Hakuin (among others), in medieval and early modern Japan.

With this book I attempt to requite the blessings of sharing the minds of these masters, along with a body and heart formed by a fierce love for the Earth and a deep intent to help forge a path that can use the latent energy of impasse and crisis (which is inherent also in koans) to open up a radical shift of direction. And I also wish to repay my debt of gratitude to all my students and teachers, especially John Tarrant, who inscribed the words "This fire runs through all things" on a *keisaku*, the ritual stick that lies on many Zen altars, and thereby became the source of all the trouble.

Lastly—a word about the haiku that appear through this book, at the end of each chapter, as capping verses set at a slight slant to the central matter of their respective chapters. They are by Ron C. Moss, an internationally recognized Tasmanian poet whose longtime Zen practice is thoroughly embedded in the marvel and fact of the natural world. Ron is also a dedicated volunteer firefighter and natural-born "first responder," and the deep fire of awareness that runs through his work and life forms the Dharma name he received from me. All of his haiku found in this book can be found in his own book, *Cloud Hands*. Here is the first one:

silence . . .
for a moment
the frogs owned it

ACKNOWLEDGMENTS

This book owes much to my teacher John Tarrant's bold innovation in removing the seal of private interaction traditionally placed on koan training. He thus released koans also into the air we breathe together and the bloodstream of everyday life, where the sharing of our dreaming minds makes clear that we cannot possibly wake up alone.

It also owes much to my indigenous Elder, Uncle Max Harrison, Dulumunmun (1937–2022), for whose unstinting and unhesitating generosity in sharing the mind of Country and the wisdom of the Dreaming with me across the decades, no adequate thanks is possible.

I thank my beloved brother, Michael, whose keen awareness and fierce defending of the exquisite natural world since earliest childhood also firmly set my path.

To each of the dozens of my brilliant Zen students across the last twenty-five years who unwittingly set about making me a teacher, my very deep gratitude. What on Earth did you think you were doing!

And in the case of this title, my very special gratitude goes to Kynan Sutherland and Deborah Chadwick for the joy of sharing a long, firelit walk through the *Record of Zhaozhou*, making it impossible for him not to get up and walk alive through the pages of this book.

To Matt Zepelin, my deep thanks for the steady, supportive clarity of his excellence as an editor that helped birth it; from here on, any errors and failings are my own.

And finally, my deepest thanks to the loving presence of David Millikan, who had my back throughout the writing of this book, despite a deep wariness of koans that virtually ensures he cannot fail to stumble into them constantly, badly stubbing his theological toes.

INTRODUCTION

Fire, Rain . . . and a Rhinoceros

In this moment, is it still possible to face the gathering darkness, and say to the physical Earth, and to all its creatures, including ourselves, fiercely and without embarrassment, I love you, and to embrace fearlessly the burning world?

—BARRY LOPEZ, "Love in a Time of Terror"

On December 31, 2019—coincidentally, the day on which the World Health Organization officially confirmed the COVID-19 pandemic—a huge crowd of silent people stood packed on a beach in southeastern Australia, facing the ocean as if waiting for deliverance. It was midday, but they massed under a sky dark as midnight. Walls of flame on three sides forced them to gather in the only place possible. Some sat and stared dumbly at the sea. Others hugged a child, a pet, or one another. Most just stood where they could, on the very narrow spit of possibility between flame and water, laboring to absorb the sheer impossibility of what was happening. Among them stood a large and beautiful, patient horse, lending a potent heraldic presence to the apocalyptic scene.

Though few among them here in comfortable Australia

thought so at the time, the disheveled people huddling under that deep umber midday sky had just joined the world's early waves of climate refugees.

That moment was five months into what would turn out to be six months of uncontrollable firestorms that slowly devoured the forests of the eastern coast of Australia in 2019 and 2020. That scene on the beach was just an hour down the road from where our household labored for days to prepare house, zendo, and land to face the thirty-seven-mile-wide megafire whose front lay just miles away, on yet one more day that fell under a newly minted weather classification: *Catastrophic Fire Danger.*

Those long months of unstoppable wildfire appeared to shock the world slightly more awake to the perils of global heating. The iron in the ash falling into the Pacific Ocean fed an algal bloom the size of the Sahara Desert. The pall of smoke visible from space punched a huge new hole in the ozone layer and circled the world three times, causing all of us to breathe the funerary remains of forests and beings, including an estimated three billion creatures, many already endangered or on the brink of extinction, as well as thirty-three people who burned to death in the fires and 450 more who died in the months of dangerously polluted air that followed. We had become very familiar with P2 masks well before COVID-19 arrived—all of us members of a species newly listed as potentially endangered.

The urgency of this book was ignited by those monster fires.

Now I find myself finishing this book in the third year of near-constant deluge. The rain that finally extinguished the fires in early 2020 dismally overstayed its welcome, going on to shatter historic annual records and previous highest flood levels, drowning towns and overwhelming tens of thousands of households. The hypersaturated soils of eastern Australia soon lost all power to absorb water and became hypoxic, beginning to drown the root systems of trees. The subtle and mysterious subsurface spring that filters through our own hillside became charged with so many tons of water that it began to melt the hillside, completely shrugging off its shoulders a long section of our main road out, first collapsing a long length of it into a sinkhole, then simply easing it down by stages into a neighboring paddock, a wonder to behold. And our seven-minute trip to town became for many months a tortuous fifty-minute mountain detour.

The signs are now plain as day, the denial of it criminal. Yet the denial itself exposes the danger peculiar to the climate crisis we face. To the extent that it goes on ambiguously and slowly enough, the sense of threat falters, even as the actual emergency steadily melts all semblance of a readable future. It may be moving at frightening speed in geophysical terms, but in human lifetime terms it can feel slow-moving enough to neutralize the word *emergency*. As long as our priorities and actions fail to match the urgency in that word, we debase its power and tacitly enable a form of doublespeak in order to accommodate both subtle and flagrant forms of denial and malignant neglect that fully intend to forestall incisive response.

———————

This book is a response to the acute alarm in human hearts that are dismayed by the world's relative failure to mount a sane response. It sets out to find how we can face this distress with a strong charge of equanimity and a skillful response. But while this discussion rides the cresting wave of a global crisis, its emerging threat has been impressed on my heart throughout the four decades in which I have also been meeting that strange category of tiny, mind-inverting fragments of discourse called the Zen koan, first as Zen student and then as a Zen teacher.

The sharp, arresting crises of the mind that lie within Zen koans have something of great value to bring to the impasse we are all now facing in the loss of climate settings to which life and civilization is currently adapted. The not-knowing mind that koans bring alive is keenly adapted to uncertainty, intimate with impasse, and adept at moving through apparent obstacle. The degree of natural affinity between koans and crisis can be placed in the service of the deep adaptation the world needs to find in this time of convulsive change. The not-knowing mind that is needed to open up koans also opens a treasury of resources for facing the climate crisis.

Koans cultivate the daring to directly meet *what is*. They offer the outrageous suggestion that we are lucky to be here in such a moment, with such a keen threat inviting us to learn to move with the speed of an awakened consciousness. And the vast bending of mind and heart that this moment in our lives is asking and will keep on asking of us, in a thousand ways and places and human beings, is deeply valuable.

Koans offer no solace to the mind that would divide the world in order to manage the pain of experience. Instead, they reveal the undivided, and in doing so they particularly resonate with the strong moment in which we find ourselves, strung as we are between profound fear and the cautious hope that human beings may yet find a liveable future.

Nor do they direct a course of action. They merely lay before us the true breadth and open nature of every moment—the "formless field of benefaction," to borrow a phrase from Zen liturgy. After that it's up to you and me. The privilege and the weight of this responsibility is great.

These initially perplexing and engaging encounter dialogues that are original to Zen turn things around by proceeding backward, upside down, or even crabwise, trusting to the empty ground of reality that is decidedly not what we *think*, but furnishes everything we *are*. And the planetary, human, and personal crises in which we find ourselves right now presents koan after koan of an essentially alive reality.

To see crisis through the eyes of a koan is to break the common frame called "problem" and instead find an opportunity to resolve a situation back into its original wholeness. For the kind of attention Zen koans require of us reclaims our existence in the physical world (and therefore its mystery), and *lets it think along with you*. Responding to crisis in a koanlike way can reveal intimate, creative, narrative, mythic, artful, playful, provocative, humorous, and fierce ways to undertake the work of defending and repairing the aliveness of the Earth.

There can be no set remedy, prescribed solution, or operating instructions for a world in crisis—only us, but more awake. We can't be held individually liable for righting the long, continuous wrong of all the factors bearing on and prolonging the climate crisis. And yet responsibility bears on us all, and most personally, for in our heart of hearts what happens and what can emerge moves only with the collective force of the words, actions, thoughts, and dreams of each of the eight billion people alive at this moment. We are sharing a huge rite of passage in facing a future that is decidedly not what it used to seem. Our crisis, however, is not a call to give up what we value most but instead, and at last, to strongly identify and become accountable to it.

The way koans break open into realization under the pressure of impasse suggest that there is a depth of realization latent in this great shared crisis. To face and engage with what is difficult and dismaying while following the promptings of a greater openness of mind and heart implicit in not-knowing holds its own strange and unexpected kind of joy, especially when we face it with others. Koans search out and can light up the field of what is trying to emerge within the great emergency of our time. Every koan explored in the pages that follow radically upturns the way we think and have thought up the place where we are, the beings that we are, and the problems we have become. Koan-adapted mind brings the fire of emptiness to meet the conflagration of the emergency, to search out the measured response hidden in the midst of turbulence, the through line in just what is happening.

And how strangely consoling it is to discover that we all share one fire of awareness, which flares in infinitely varied forms of sentience, experience, expression, color, shape, imagination, feeling, gesture, birth, and death.

KOANS AND CRISIS HEAL EACH OTHER

Koans and crisis both yield to the approach of the not-knowing mind and glimpse the fullness of reality that the thinking mind and business-as-usual hurry past.

Most of the English-speaking world's familiarity with koans has come through the Japanese Zen tradition, but Zen is an adaptation of a much older Chinese Buddhist school known as Chan, which has deep connections to Daoism. Zen's Daoist rootstock easily recognized the emptiness wisdom of Mahayana Buddhism as it arrived over centuries from China to India. And so Daoism seamlessly accepted the graft of Buddhism, to become Chan. Those Daoist roots of Chan and Zen are deep in the Earth and at home on the planet, at ease with the flow of the natural world.

The first signs of the spirited form of engagement with sentient reality that in time became the paradoxical form that is koan (from *kō*, "public," and *an*, commonly rendered in Chan and Zen as "case") rose in the speech and actions of a generation or two of eighth-century Chan masters, including Shitou Xiqian (700–790) and Mazu Daoyi (709–788). Their lively encounters with people, later gathered into what became koan records and koan collections, were responses to the intense crises of eighth-century Tang dynasty China. Great teachers like Mazu were surviving and making do in an inchoate, collapsed world. They functioned in the wake of a twenty-year period of extraordinary violence and societal collapse that followed what became known as the An Lushan Rebellion (755–763), in which a general by that name attempted to install a counter (Yan) dynasty at vast cost to the viability of the entire world of China. Census records across that period imply a huge death toll—through war, looting, devastation of towns and croplands, mass starvation, and disease—of somewhere between thirteen million and thirty-one million souls. As the largest single atrocity to that point in human history, it was comparable in generational impact to the two world wars of the twentieth century.

What later became known as Zen's treasury of koans could reasonably be compared to a rising immune response and potent medicine for a time of disintegration and collapse. These sometimes wildly demonstrative "public cases"—gong-an or kung-an in Chinese, koan in Japanese—directly enacted the walking clear of self and all preemptive knowings, letting people tap into all that opens to the not-knowing mind. Each koan is an open offer to share the benefaction of the mind that sees emptiness, which runs like fire through all things, including you and me. And to see that what is timeless, formless, unborn, and ablaze in each particle of matter, in each moment, is us, when you finally notice that it is.

Thus koans emerged as part of the response of Shitou, Mazu, and other eighth-century practitioners to a world riven, like ours, by war and societal collapse. As the eighth-century Chinese poet Du Fu reflected in "Gazing at Spring," "The nation is shattered, mountains and rivers remain." But not until our time have koans needed to meet a planetary disaster, a ruined natural world—and the indigestible fact that it is all our own work.

SAVE THE EARTH

Nobody can live somewhere in general, though much of our digital culture might like to persuade us we can. Every breath from first to last is breathed somewhere in particular. Earth made us, wakes us, resolves us into its fullness. To overlook this and to relate only vaguely to where you live is to place your living place in peril.

Inevitably in our time of climate tragedy, religions (at last) are slowly beginning to turn their gaze from personal salvation to saving the planet. In the context of Buddhism, terms like *ecodharma*, *ecosattva*, and *engaged Buddhism* have emerged as prompts to stir the practitioner beyond the goal of personal fulfillment to collective action. But in an ecological crisis that has no analogue in recorded history, there's a heightened urgency—felt and addressed throughout this book—to realize the Dharma of self and Earth healing more deeply into each other.

The great thirteenth-century Japanese Zen master Dogen echoes this call when he says, "When you know the place where you are, practice begins." He's not speaking of familiarity with your surroundings. He's saying there's no practice at all until you realize the true nature of *where* you are as being not one jot separate from *what* you are. Zen's deep inquiry into the self is a merciful dissolving of what you are into all that is. It would now be simply untenable—under the pressure of a planetary crisis that reaches right to the foundations of life—to separate Zen's nonpartisan study of the self (which by nature becomes a deeply healing forgetting of the self) from the place where we are, the time that we're in, and the thoroughly earthy reality of our essential nature.

The great Indigenous wisdom traditions, founded as they are in a richly earthed oral literacy of place, offer an invaluable template for such an Earth Dharma. That human beings can—indeed, must—consciously seek congruence with the ecological wholeness of natural systems is held as a sacred fact by traditional peoples, and this view opens the way for us here. Zen's experience of an alive, interconnected reality finds many points of resonance with the desire at the base of all indigenous wisdom to heal the gap we attempt to force between ourselves and the Earth, as I explore in chapter 6.

That self and Earth healed back into each other is the most fertile ground for all forms of acting on behalf of the Earth is the premise of this book; every part of it is an embodied meditation on this possibility, coming alive in every koan taken up in these pages.

THE KOAN OF DEEP ADAPTATION

In 2018, a long, thoughtful, and deeply pessimistic essay by British sustainability expert Jem Bendell went viral. Titled "Deep Adaptation," it strongly influenced Extinction Rebellion, a UK-based environmental activist movement, which was formed the same year that Bendell's essay was published and continues to influence global activism and thinking about the climate crisis.[1]

Bendell's essay broke through the wall of spurious hope and wary optimism behind which we've been hiding for decades, forcing us to face the fact that the time we have to mitigate runaway global warming has been tragically squandered. This leaves us needing to "unearth" in ourselves a new capacity to adapt to the convulsive effects of such rapid change. Deep adaptation is not just surviving disaster, but transforming ourselves within and through the demanding circumstances it imposes on us. The term implies that relinquishing normal expectations, repairing what has and is being so damaged, and facilitating regenerative capacities in systems is our sole path of not just surviving, but flourishing as a species. But the "deep" in his phrase reaches also to the spiritual depth and basis of this planetary crisis.

To his surprise, Bendell found that asking people in a supportive community context to seriously consider collapse as inevitable, catastrophe as probable, and extinction as possible did not deepen apathy and depression, but instead raised a communal energy of connection, creativity, and an even stronger caring. He also came to see that deep adaptation must reach not just to Earth's physical changes and our enhanced ecological intelligence, but right to the psychological, philosophical, and spiritual grounds of what it means to be human. This requires us to address some important questions: How can we keep what we know matters most? What must we let go of so we don't make matters worse? And what can we bring back to help meet the coming difficulties and tragedies?

At the time it was published, Bendell's essay marked the end of his willingness as a sustainability expert to talk about deferring or even successfully halting what is already fully underway as accelerated warming and weather extremes. At the time there was no concerted political response appearing anywhere on the horizon, just more of the unconvincing blandishments, manufactured doubt, bad-faith statements, commercial greenwashing, targets devoid of plans, protests of innocence, blatant lies, and perhaps worst of all, crushing silence from all the obvious holders of political and economic power. Four or five years since then, public awareness and activism is visibly rising, and the almost shockingly rapid reduction in the cost of wind and solar energy has started to leave fossil fuel assets looking stranded in the near future, even as war in Europe has weaponized existing dependence on fossil fuel supplies once more, forcing energy prices back up. The complex whole of what is happening must be acknowledged and held in mind, and we must relinquish our expectations of a return to normalcy along with the almost equally seductive tendency to catastrophize.

Blind hope lies too close to moral complacency; blind despair is moral abdication. But between hope and despair extends a broad field of moral integrity, and it is there that a match can be struck between what you most deeply hold as valuable and what you do to let your actions make that clear.

RELINQUISHMENT

Deep adaptation turns inevitably, almost severely, toward relinquishment, for however slow we are to give up our customary expectations, a planetary climate crisis has already begun their fire sale. At the heart of deep adaptation is the not-knowing mind and its liberating self-relinquishment. Such self-relinquishment comes to bear in every koan, but the urgency of the present crisis tells us that we must learn this skill even while we endure the tragic loss of intact landscapes that are impossibly dear to our hearts, watching them undergo painful transformation.

Relinquishment, then, means giving up expectations of all kinds. Not-knowing, in the Zen sense, can seem as simple (and demanding) as stepping back time and time again from the habit of letting what you believe you know swiftly steal the bare fresh moments of this life and replace them with a kind of forgery. This process goes deep and entails dropping an unquestioned sense of who and what you are. That dropping away can be liberatingly joyful, but also seriously discomfiting, even alarming. For the sense of self rests in a rarely examined habitual pursuit of preferences that flatter, comfort, protect, and continually fortify its fragile edifice. Some tough grit in the rice or sharp thorns in the sand lie waiting here. Every consumer choice must now be weighed against climate chaos; every decision must be examined in light of the world we are leaving to the generations who follow. The pressure builds to un-choose comforts that cost the Earth simply too much, to abandon bland hope devoid of action, and to drop all self-deceiving trust in some undreamt-of technological fix that will happily ensure that nothing needs to seriously change after all.

The relinquishment to be faced by those already primed by strong anger and alarm about the climate can be to forsake being so very "right," in order to glimpse how much that narrows the field, limits the company you can share, and is by nature—in a universe of unceasing change—always already edging into being "wrong." Relinquishment also can mean sitting and truly being with the aching discomfort and fatigue of enduring the many dissonances of our age. It means holding in your own body all the many factors of ecological breakdown and the human suffering it entails, while also attending to the immediate, mundane needs of life, which are so difficult to unstitch from what is causing the climate crisis. The burden of this can dull response, and the shame of failing to respond can collapse into an irritable, fearful wish to escape at all costs.

But there's a fearless generosity in not-knowing: the willingness to doubt the talking mind, and the ability to trust your most fundamental self, form one dynamic. Not-knowing begins with doubting that the self is an independent "something" carved out from the whole. This is the first wall of the mind coming down, and more can follow. As the Heart Sutra puts it, "With no walls in the mind, no walls and therefore no fear, far beyond delusive thinking, right here is nirvana." Instead of withdrawing for safety and falling back defensively on what fear believes you know, the not-knowing mind leans on what is compounded in your flesh and bones by every experience of joy and well-placed trust you've ever had. Taking that together with curiosity toward whatever is happening in the present moment, you will find something far more interesting than what walled-in fear can glimpse.

The walls in the mind are coming down; there is air to breathe once more, signs of life reappear all around, and a new register of understanding has a chance to form.

ONLY TO LIVE

As with any koan or any crisis, climate breakdown is our chance to experience resolving the constant and largely unpredictable changes with which we are living, with something that is unchanging and always at rest. The chance to affirm, as the late U.S. Poet Laureate W. S. Merwin, a longtime student of Zen, pointed out,

> We were not born to survive
> Only to live[2]

Merwin's *only to live* is fortunately too wide to have edges, as this book explores throughout its pages. It is this self that is no longer separate and standing alone, but gathered in and companioned, naturally seeking greater congruence with what is unfolding.

The first and last relinquishment is the knowing that replaces direct experience. Not-knowing practices imposing nothing or as little as possible on what is happening, so as to experience things directly, just as they undeniably are, comfortable or not, and it practices making this the natural (because most interesting and informative) choice. Adaptation begins in accepting every offer and moving with what is happening, as in the example of the fourteenth-century Japanese Zen master Daito Kokushi, who, though named as National Teacher by the emperor, was eccentric and unroofed enough sometimes to choose the life of a beggar under a bridge. Finding himself caught short once in a deluge, he wrote a verse simply announcing (or confirming) the situation:

> No umbrella?
> I'll use the rain as my raincoat!

There's no winning or losing in this. When you can no more say where you begin or end than a breaking wave, a wider path of action opens, both softened and strengthened by the fearlessness and resilience of the not-knowing mind.

With relinquishment the other facets of deep adaptation open as the fascinatingly detailed repair and restoration work undertaken to regenerate whatever ensures and sustains life. This requires strong community-oriented engagement and unheroic kinds of "doings" that, as with any ecological system, are mutual, emergent, and distributed among the many at every point. In small moments and large, the same intent underlies the great work of bringing human minds and the behemoth of ecological collapse to a point where they can begin to heal each other, and the climate juggernaut can be slowed and directed toward new equilibrium, and eventual regeneration.

Every koan brings the mind to a stop in order to glimpse what stays obscured and unseen in the forward rush of intensely narrow human knowings. Every koan is a life-restoring heresy to the type of mind that works by carving what is seamless into opposable parts. Sometimes referred to as "Dharma gates," koans offer the way back home to the intelligence of the undivided mind, through gates that have a very decided-looking front to them, but no back at all.

In seeking a foundation for the long walk of deep adaptation ahead of us, Bendell not only acknowledges the vital importance of indigenous wisdom still alive in the world, he also reaches out to the resource that lies in Thich Nhat Hanh's thoroughly Zen teaching on interbeing, which implies: I can be here because you are here. Your life is also my life. If I go down inside myself far enough, I come up in you. And that "you" is not limited to other human beings but lies wide open to any detail of this sentient Earth and the cosmos in which she swims.

To the extent that we get past ourselves, we find how deeply we inter-are. All responsiveness to the climate crisis begins here. Its soulfulness depends on facing the "other" and realizing "no other." Poet Gary Snyder said that our soul is our dream of the other—in other words, how we hold otherness in our hearts and let it inform and magnify the response of this heart. This interbeing is a very tender, stretching kind of business.

THE INTELLIGENCE OF EMPTINESS

So, koan wisdom and the practice of deep adaptation are approached throughout this book by way of the resolving intelligence of not-knowing. Neuroscience has verified some of the benefits of cultivating a not-knowing mind (using terms such as "releasing concepts" or "practicing bare attention") in meditation and mindfulness practice: a measurable decrease in anxiety, depression, and obsessive patterns of thinking and feeling, as well as a lifting of creative potency and confirmed feelings of greater spaciousness and ease. All of these are welcome indeed, but here I am more intent on exploring the forensic capacity of the not-knowing mind to meet the koan that is our climate crisis—and how doing so helps create a path for a skillful and effective response both individually and collectively.

The practice of not-knowing has no intellectual woolliness about it. On the contrary, it enriches critical inquiry into the extraordinarily layered nature of what we are facing at this time. It does so by slowing the metabolism of the mind down to where it can rest even in conflicted complexity and bring curiosity to bear, unmoved by immediate, reactive certainty. In not-knowing introspection, the practical, ethical, spiritual, and political currents of thought that must all coalesce to shape calm, critical awareness have a chance to discover well-founded intuitive moves of contemplative thought and action.

The not-knowing mind is noncontentious in temperament.

It proceeds with wonder and curiosity, and at a speed that allows the world more easily to come forward, unguarded. Zen koans foster not-knowing as our most valuable and intimate default posture of mind—an informing stance that shifts the self from the foreground to the background, immeasurably widening the view. The not-knowing mind can best intuit where the opening lies in a tight situation and inform the way you hold and share authority and offer care. It engineers no final answers, but changes fundamentally what actions, speech, and thought can be found to rebalance the scale and open the way in each situation.

The not-knowing at the core of Zen koan practice upends and turns things around to reveal the implicit but unasked questions that can radically open the ground from which we can proceed. It's work that is never done and never boring, as it always stays open to the mystery that lies deeper than words, the fire that runs through all things. As the Persian lyric poet Hafez advised, "Start seeing everything as God, but keep it a secret." Not-knowing is the decision to let reality become clear to you unforced; to sit and walk in a way that is permeable to silence and wonder, letting it resolve and inform you even as it moves you most simply to act.

In recent years some of my students took to reworking an old Zen koan "Save a ghost!" as "Save the Earth!" Who is saved from ghostliness as a species when we begin to move in accord with the Earth, to share her mind and feel her suffering as our own? From this vantage, the deep adaptation needed in order to save ourselves becomes less of a problem to be solved and more of a continuing realization as to who we really are. It also holds out no promise that this process should be comfortable, easy, or ever complete.

And it needs us to ask: How ready are we to suffer planetary healing? And how ready are we to concede the self in order to save the Earth from ourselves? We are that deep idea of the

Earth to examine herself in ourselves, to look back at the universe, back at the miracle of existence. How willing are we to be torn into a greater and more enduring wholeness with the Earth, then, as she suffers the changes we are inflicting? Let's now trial a few more koans that usefully provoke a course of deep adaptation.

OF DONKEYS AND WELLS

The "old well," like the "ancient mirror," is a traditional image of the brimming emptiness that looks back at you from every form when you see with eyes of emptiness. In Case 52 of Hongzhi's collection of 100 koans, titled *The Book of Equanimity*, we find Zen master Caoshan (840–901) asking Elder De how he would like to explain the correspondence of emptiness and form—often pictured as the moon's equal, nonpartisan reflection in every ripple and droplet of water.

Elder De volunteers, "It is like a donkey looking at a well."

Caoshan comments, "Nicely expressed, but only 80 percent of the matter."

Elder De asks, "How about you, Acharya?"

Caoshan says, "It is like a well looking at a donkey."

Elder De leans on the side of the donkey (you, me) gazing with not-knowing into the brimming well of emptiness, ardently offering "I'm all yours" for the life-restoring shock of seeing for ourselves that "Form is emptiness."

Caoshan, not discounting this for a moment, nevertheless leans on the side of emptiness looking quite naturally through our own awake eyes, emptiness following our every move exactly, inseparably from us, confirming "I'm all yours" as our realized state of "Emptiness is form."

This koan poses a searching question to every moment of this life. What does emptiness see, even in this searing, anguished moment of reckoning that we all share now? Opening the koan in the direction of our self-created ecocrisis, we can take the seemingly inexhaustible well to be this vast planetary ecosystem, from which no one is excluded and nothing can be lost or gained; unfolding in time and yet timelessly distributed across infinite points of sentience; functioning everywhere and at once and so with no singular center . . . or self. Now the "well" is clearly looking searchingly back at us. What do we look like in its gaze? What is it to regard ourselves with its eyes?

Putting aside all dismissal of donkeys (who are entirely citizens above suspicion), in "A donkey looks at a well" it's hard not to feel our befuddled human world staring mutely at the vast, fulsome complexity of Earth's life systems, which we've barely begun to plumb. And with "A well looks at a donkey," the tremendous pathos of the central question of our times, together with the great wide Earth, begins to gaze deeply into us, laying bare our way of living by damage, and our every attempt to stand apart from the seamless whole of life (as though every breath we draw did not completely rely on and affirm it). Creatures, alive Earth, and something deep in us as well, watching us closely. When will we notice what is?

The longer you look deep into the ancient mirror of the natural world, the harder it is to find in our vast, hot, carbon-fueled world resilience, longevity, sustenance, or a self you are proud to own up to, and the harder it becomes to avoid seeing our world to be a vain proposition with no sustainable basis—a chimera, increasingly difficult to call real when placed against actual leaves, grass, rocks, rivers, and creaturely life.

When the well looks back at the donkey, you can't help but recognize every detail of this Earth as continuous with this self, including even half-baked human beings. Donkey and well discover each other in each other, laying out for us the beautiful work of becoming more human and awake. Both are blessed. Is this one? Two?

Plainly, deep adaptation can only be found in according more closely with the deep ideas of the Earth. As an ancient Chinese saying warns, "You can move cities, but you cannot move wells." There's a given for the project of deep adaptation right there.

A poem by Ikkyu Sojun (1394–1481)—the eccentric, iconoclastic Japanese Zen monk and poet—is also taken up in many places as a miscellaneous koan to look into this same mysterious well: "In a well that has never been dug, water ripples from a stream that does not flow. Someone, with no shadow or form, is drawing the water."

Let yourself into the presence of this mysterious "someone." They have no problem, in the great dream of this Earth, in moving their limbs, drawing the water, and drinking it with gusto, using the whole great matter of being here wonderfully well. Look closely and notice that every miraculous drop of water on Earth ripples from "a well that has never been dug." That water ripples out (as we do) from the timeless and empty "stream that does not flow." Complete and at rest in every ripple.

The question rippling throughout this book is who is that "someone," and how do they draw and use this wonderful water in aid and defense of the Earth? For interbeing is not just a noun to name the true state of reality; it is also its verb.

HANDS AND EYES ALL OVER THE BODY

You can catch a glimpse of the mysterious activity of Thich Nhat Hanh's interbeing in a koan drawn from the magisterial *Blue Cliff Record*, another of the great collections of koans.

Two Zen worthies, Yunyan and Daowu, are talking about Guanyin (Kuan Yin, or Avalokitesvara), the bodhisattva of compassion, who is often depicted with many arms radiating from her shoulders, in every open hand an open eye of realization.

Yunyan asks Daowu, "How does the Bodhisattva of Great Compassion use those many hands and eyes?"

Daowu responds, "It's like someone reaching back, groping for a pillow in the middle of the night."

Yunyan says, "I understand."

Daowu asks, "How do you understand it?"

Yunyan replies, "All over the body are hands and eyes."

Daowu says, "You have said quite a bit there, but you've only said 80 percent of it." Yunyan is obliging: "What do you say, Elder Brother?"

Daowu says, "Throughout the body are hands and eyes."[3]

These two are working with the questions of how compassion is actualized, where it subsists, what its deep nature is, and how it manifests. What does a compassionate response look like? As simple and natural as "It's like someone reaching for a pillow in the middle of the night," says Daowu. This strikes me as a beautiful suggestion, offering a vision of compassion as a state of such ease that it puts everything else a little more effortlessly at ease. But don't mistake *ease* for *easy*; this deep state of intimacy draws on a strong kind of charge laid willingly on the self. And don't miss *the middle of the night*, here: the darkness of not-knowing, an almost complete absence of self-consciousness, is fundamental to that ease.

The next two suggestions offered to each other, "All over the body are hands and eyes" and "Throughout the body are hands and eyes," allow us to see how interbeing looks to not-knowing eyes, and how completely everything moves together as one body of being.

As for "all over" and "throughout," are they really splitting hairs here, or are we just being asked to leave our hairsplitting equipment at the door?

In any case, it's a brilliant evocation not just of compassion, but of ecological wholeness. This "body," of course, includes you, even as it opens to the interconnectedness of all sentient life, the entire sentient planet, all reaching along with you for that pillow in the middle of the night, as crisis closes around us.

Those hands and eyes are also yours and mine, responding to the cries of the world as Guanyin is said to do. But how naturally they do so, with no "me" or "you" standing in the way. As for the 80 percent, once more—even this half-finished breath is the whole of it, along with the half-formed thoughts and the slight stumbles of the mind. It is undivided and can never stop opening, and every "part" of opening is the whole of it.

Clearly there's love running through all interbeing; that seems written in the nature of this earthly reality as well as inscribed on our very bones. Ikkyu laughed at the way priests minutely pored over the Dharma and endlessly chanted complicated sutras while failing to first learn how to read what he called "the love letters sent by the wind and rain, the snow and the moon."[4]

Dharma is the Earth and the universe speaking directly in human terms; koans, which each touch the absolute nature of reality right at the nerve center of the relative world, are its utterances in the midst of life. The absolute of emptiness is a fire that runs through all things, burning up "difference." But equally its fire is silently at rest in every unrepeatable form that appears and endures under the law of change. The frog glistens with completeness; so does the pebble, the scales on the snake, the knuckles of your hand, or the way your skin grows warm in the sun.

Let us take them up and use them freely, in service of a fierce love for the Earth.

———

Throughout this book, expect a deep encounter with the reality of climate change, our rightfully intense feelings about it, and the vital question of how we can respond to its vast implications. To prepare the ground, part 1 explores the nature of the self, koan mind, Zen meditation, and the undazzled intelligence of emptiness that is not-knowing.

Any effective engagement with practical climate change action springs from a fundamental question that at first glance seems pointedly oblique to the crisis: what is this self? But to question and break open the dream of the self is to find the remarkable tipping point in consciousness that lies latent in the question, and latent in this crisis, waiting for us to discover the medicine in the sickness, the healing in the suffering.

Until "self" is held as a live question rather than its own unquestioned answer, we're stuck with looking on semi-passively from the outside, hoping for successfully engineered solutions to the problem of convulsive climate change, while all the time oblivious to the fact that we're swimming in a reality with no outside to it, an ocean of transformative energy.

A sense of self is a practical necessity, but it is possible to live a life unaware of how much it can constrict the heart and block the light, leaving us unaware of the bigger picture of the current crisis, even as we struggle to act passionately within it. Without holding the self as a question, we're caught short of the full potential of our intense feelings about the suffering Earth.

Parts 2 and 3 flesh out the ways in which this separate sense of self can heal back into awareness of all beings and the whole Earth. Part 3 in particular looks respectfully into the affinities between Zen mind and the subtle template of a fully Earthed understanding offered to the world in the indigenous wisdom of Aboriginal Australia. To reinstate the value of indigenous knowledge is not to imply or to urge a return to a mode of life prior to vast historic change; it is to temper the mind of a breakneck world back into greater congruence with the terms of the Earth. It is to learn what we have lost or shoved aside, and to restore access to an ecological base of knowledge that is imaginatively whole with all that lives, and that rests in kinship between all people and beings and the Earth herself. Then, daring to ride the tiger of climate crisis can become a way of moving together with the Earth and all her beings while seeking more sustainable congruence with one another.

And rather than being a task at which one might succeed or fail, Zen's prompting of a healing crisis is an open process with no predetermined end point. Undisturbed by our mortality and supported by clouds, children, grass, stories, silence, rivers, your broken thumbnail (and the half-moon rim of dirt behind it)—all of them impermanent, yet also complete, and sharing something empty and eternal—we find that what we seek is always here.

To all such things we are each sole heir. Each bright thing suggests it is good to be in a living human body at this time. And when zazen is deep, it requires effort to wish for any kind of elsewhere. The Earth's welcome is so direct and plain, as plain as the weird, unhomely indifference offered to it in modern times by our strange species. Just as though we might be extra-terrestrials.

And now let me place at the head of this book three great koans, two of them from *The Blue Cliff Record*, that form the archway through which the logic of crisis and no-crisis flows.

Its capstone koan, which structures the three parts into which this book is divided, is Case 87, "Yunmen's Medicine and Sickness." Yunmen Wenyan (864–949) says, "Medicine and sickness heal each other. The whole Earth is medicine. Then what is this self?"

These words stand like blasts from a shofar. All you can do is submit to them and see who you turn out to be as they resonate with your entire life. The medicine is found in the sickness, the healing begins in realizing the empty fullness of the whole great Earth, and the turning-point of that healing lies in resolving "What is this self?"

———

The second koan also comes from the record of Yunmen. He quotes the words of his teacher, Xuefeng Yicun (822–908), who said, "All the buddhas of the past, present, and future are turning the great wheel over the blazing fire." But he quotes these words only to turn them around, saying, "Rather, the blazing fire is expounding the Dharma to all the buddhas of the three times, and they are standing on the ground and listening."

The nature of that blazing fire is taken up throughout this book and is the business of every koan examined. Yunmen reverses the angle of view in Xuefeng's words and shifts it toward the perspective of Caoshan's declaration that "the well is looking at a donkey." But he goes further and lets the fire that runs through all things actively expound the Dharma to all the buddhas of the three times, leaving them respectfully *standing on the Earth and listening*. The affinity here with the flow of Australian indigenous respect law, taken up in part 3, is striking. There is a uniquely Aboriginal use of the English word *Country* in Australia, in which use is lodged a rich and subtle lifelong healing conversation with the Earth. Like the reversal in Yunmen's koan, that conversation reverses the flow of knowing, and aligns with Zen in requiring a deeply alert and humanly embodied no-self to stand entire with the Earth, both feet on the ground, and to listen with every sinew of our being.

As Dogen says, with words that reverberate throughout this book, "When you know the place where you are, practice begins." And not until.

———

Finally, it is always an interesting moment when a rhinoceros turns up.

The third koan that pokes its horn throughout this book to skewer our attention is Case 91 in *The Blue Cliff Record*, "Yanguan's Rhinoceros Fan." I freely admit to turning to this koan to meet not just the vital possibility of waking up a little more but also—and not separately—the call of deep adaptation to repair and regenerate what is broken on the living Earth in this very moment.

One day, Yanguan Qian (750–842) called to his attendant, saying, "Bring me the rhinoceros fan."

The product specifications of this mysterious object are lost, but imagine a fan with a rhinoceros horn handle that's been extracted from a once-living and complete rhinoceros, its unique keratin horn removed and repurposed into just one more thing extracted from the tissue of the living Earth for trivial human use.

The attendant says, "I can't. It's broken." Who knows how cagey was this fellow who professes to be able to find no further trace of a separate self?

But Yanguan is as present, unaccountable, and complete as an old rhino. He sets the task for a world in which something as astonishing as a planetary climate hospitable to numberless teeming forms of life can get taken, broken, ruined, forsaken, and tragically lost to the generations.

"If the fan is broken, then bring me the rhinoceros!" he instructs us all.

That's our job. And there's no way out of it. Bringing back the rhinoceros—or if you please, the planet, the living world, as well as the human being—in a more awakened state, entire with reality, is the purpose of this book.

> red moon eclipse
> a mosquito settles
> on my bloodline

Part One

A TIPPING POINT IN CONSCIOUSNESS

Medicine and sickness heal each other.
The whole Earth is medicine.
Then what is this self?

—YUNMEN

A monk asked Zhaozhou, "What is meditation?"
"It's not meditation," the master replied.
"Then what is it?" asked the monk.
"It's alive," said Zhaozhou. "It's *alive!*"

火

1

WHAT IS THIS SELF?

How laughable, that someone comes to grab the tiger's whiskers!

—XUEDOU

SOMEONE

This strange, familiar, yet unearthly sense of self, this "someone" . . .

Like Flat Earth Society members, we give the illusion of the self our absolute conviction. We need a self to "get around in" successfully; other people also need us to have it, in a sound, coherent, and available state. Deeply involving as it can be, is it indefinitely interesting? Do you really want to take it with you when you go?

Always trying to assert its presence, under scrutiny this self is nevertheless hard to find, a chameleon of changeability within its ever-shifting circumstances. It can grow wildly incoherent and lost, making you dangerous to yourself and the people around you. And though apparently anchored in a body you call your own, is it solid?

There was a time when you knew yourself to be recognized

and completely accepted by the waves, the grass, other creatures, clouds, stars, hillsides, rocks, wind, music. Mountains would smile in recognition and trees returned your salute. You had no thought of distinguishing your being from all that is, while also being a distinct organism pledged to stay alive, identify danger, and avoid death. Both truths somehow coalesced into the "I" that gradually carves itself out of the seamless world.

No wonder the vast elaboration called the self is so very strange and incongruous, and leaves us with the sense that we are poignantly alone on the Earth. This self and its subtly estranged state on the Earth is itself a koan, a matter to be resolved, a peace to be found, a deep agreement to be reached, a perfect fit to be revealed, and . . . a grave to be climbed out of.

THE TEARS OF SLEEPING BIRDS

Every koan is predicated on the koan of this self, effectively asking, "What is it?" And every koan asks us to get past the self enough to glimpse our essential reality—unadorned, unmediated, unqualified, and undivided—not as a plane of life floating above all exigencies, but the discoverable source of our own real presence within all exigencies.

Zen's temperament is sane, realistic, playful, and rigorous, and it is loving beyond all sentimentality. This is exactly what gives it great imaginative access to the subtle, underground rivers of wisdom that have been tapped throughout the koan tradition—great medicine indeed for a world of such deep private unease and civilizational disease. Keizan Jokin (1268–1325) was a student of Dogen's direct students and became known as the second great founder of the Soto Zen school in Japan. He left us the following verse to Case 43 of *Transmissions of the Light*, which invites us into the deeply playful movement of koan mind:

The moon of mind, the flower of eyes,
opening since time beyond kalpas,
are bright and beautiful.
Who will play with them?

"The flower of eyes"—well, that's laid out before your senses. Awake, nothing is hidden, all things are alive and pollinating this mind. "Enlightenment is the intimacy of all things," as Dogen puts it, and all things hold nothing back. All things are so intimately interconnected and sharing themselves, such that there is no gap. But "the moon of mind"? Why does the mind at home in emptiness find its image in the cool fire of the moon?

"Moon" does a lot of work in Zen. It sails through the empty sky of the mind, needing no support. It slims down to nothing and darkens completely. It grows full and complete, and in that equitable moonlight of no color, each thing equally holds up the moon, distinct, and yet also not so much. Hard edges go. "Moon" becomes the neutral, nonpartisan character of each thing it illuminates. And you can gaze into that light directly, without flinching, without harm, without dazzling yourself. Notice how you grow still under the moon as its lumens and your own eyes actualize each other—the eyes of the moon. And on certain occasions, the shadow of Earth turns the moon blood red.

Little wonder that in Zen, a tradition hard on words and that does not turn willingly toward explanations, the full, radiant moon is a stand-in for realization.

The fierce, unmodulated, absolute light of the sun, on the other hand, will not be looked at. It pins your eyes, an insistent weight on your shoulders, forcing all shadows under their trees at midday, tending life with warmth and endangering it with heat waves. The solitary brightness of the moon, however, silently and completely reflects that absolute light in a form that returns your relaxed, undazzled gaze. A moment of moon contemplation is a silent era. Each distinct thing is confirmed in its silvered still-ness, all things equal under the moon. Every droplet holds the moon complete. Shatter the water, and the moon steadily re-forms. Even racing through clouds, the moon is unperturbed. It is untroubled by its waxing and waning, which is like breathing, like life, eternal yet at home in calm impermanence, darkening in not-knowing, growing brilliant in realization. The light of the moon confirms the darkness of the empty sky.

With the steady "moon of mind" clarifying itself by all that flows through the senses as the "flower of eyes," Earth's crisis can be ap-proached as a strangely privileged moment to be sharply alive, on call, awake to the Earth, prepared to meet what is unfolding as in-separable from ourselves. The reasons to feel Earth's distress arrive daily now, like the deepest rumblings of elephant love calls, inau-dible yet received directly in the bones that lodge the heart. What scares you so deeply? Could it be a love cry from the Earth, earth-ing you, urging you back "home" to this interconnected reality?

Caller on a podcast: "What do you mean by *interconnected?*" Pause, then the podcast guest, an ecologist, responds: "There is a species of moth in Madagascar that drinks the tears of sleeping birds."

SELF MAY BE HIDING SELF

In Botswana, some railroad crossings bear a wonderful sign that says WARNING: Trains May Be Hiding Trains. Likewise, the method of zazen is both hidden and revealed entirely in the act, and then goes further to reveal the birdsong hiding in the bird-song, mountains hidden in mountains, and original self hiding (for now) in this self.

Zazen just studies the embodied mind with a relaxed, undi-vided gaze, allowing the radical question "What is this self?" to come alive in us as it will, sometimes by infinite stealth, other times with a tiger's roar. In a typically low-key undoing of expectations, Zen calls our clear, original, and most natural experience "ordinary mind."

In zazen, ordinary things grow plainer and stranger at once. Ordinary does not mean ho-hum or customary. It means ordinary the way a bee softly bothers the flowers, ordinary (and equally strange) as your toes, mysterious as a baby's smile or as waves welling and sucking back over rocks. It means as ordinary and unlikely as the overwhelming fact of the universe, of breathing in and out, of having an unbounded consciousness that seems also to have a name and history and to belong to a familiar mortal body.

Ordinary means able to be with what is, freely moving with circumstances, at ease everywhere like a leaf on the breeze, as the eighth-century master Layman Pang wished to be. Zazen is focused investigation of the mysterious nature of the self as it grows gradually transparent to what is, not by directing oneself toward something special, rather by just (just!) noticing and gently abandoning all alternatives to unadorned being, sitting, and breathing. It begins in sitting and grounding the mind in the bare fact of body and breath.

Simple. And so it takes all that we are, and for as long as we have while still aboveground.

A TWIG, SNAPPING

Settling in this way gradually involves inhabiting a more seamless breath-body-mind. Slowly, thoughts diminish and a willing state of no-mind takes its place.

This is not a blank mind, but quietly very alive. When by its own grace mind is no longer restlessly reaching for anything at all—some utterly ordinary sound, sight, or touch, a sudden bird remarking, a twig snapping, a flame flickering, a shadow melting in the grass, the way the wall meets the floor, the human cry of a sneeze, the crunch of an apple in your mouth, the sizzling of a pan on the fire—the entire universe comes to light as not other than yourself, clean as a whistle, far beyond complications.

Such a coup de grâce is party to your gradual or sudden yielding to the nonpartisan completeness of each moment. Calling it enlightenment implies something forever settled; it's not. Sometimes settled, sometimes unsettled, it is actually just the start of realizing what lies beyond explanation, which has recognized and included you completely, at last.

Where did this mysterious being come from? What is it? Who breathes? What is this self? Where does this it begin or end? With no goal or method or dream of conclusive answers, zazen comes alive with something bigger, more generous, and infinitely more promising than an eternally separate self could ever dream up. The full tiger, in fact.

Nothing is hidden. Whales, blue wrens, cries in the dark, the sudden soft thud of a heavy camellia—each thing steps forward to confirm how mysterious this business of your being here really is. Koan mind lifts not-knowing to a more acute state, but zazen is itself a round and ever-opening koan, a matter to be resolved. This is not the same as sitting and thinking about a great question. It's simply the vast, open disposition of "What is this?" and "Who is this?" realizing itself breath by embodied breath.

TEACHING THE MIND TO SIT

You begin by sitting down in the middle of the universe. You offer yourself just as though the mystery that is you already belongs, and belongs so entirely to the entire cosmos that you gradually lose even the burden of your own name. A poised, alert mind assumes nothing, objects to nothing. When you choose not to object to what is, it has a much harder time becoming objectionable. And when you drop each niggling impulse to control or engineer your mind for outcomes, things as they are can finally meet and heal the fugitive, never-quite-willing-to-be-here self, who agreed to sit down and at least give it a good go.

Breath is the broker of this peace of wanting nothing found within the not-knowing of what this self is. You settle with a natural, upright spine free of straining for anything. With your weight thus earthed and settled, head erect, your chin is slightly tucked in so as to center the weight of your head on your neck, and your eyes are slightly open and unfocused or gently closed, lightly aware of every stage of breath swelling in and flowing out. You need quiet persistence in letting thoughts become mere background to your attention, which rests in the breath and in hearing and feeling your whole body.

Gradually, sounds, sensations, emotions, half-thoughts passing through are noticed and accepted, but all entirely equally in equanimity, with nothing to prefer and nothing to reject. Inside and outside equalize in one flow. Edges disappear. Success or failure disappears, and something familiar and marvelously ordinary resumes its natural place.

Just being. Nothing needed. Nothing added. Nothing missing. Natural, as in sharing the actual nature of all things, which includes you completely. Impulses subside, and that feels not odd, but strangely promising.

"What about when the mind neither stops nor moves on?" a monk asks Zhaozhou.

"It's alive!" Zhaozhou confirms. Deeply alive, in that not-knowing state.

The most alive and present state of mind dwells right on the point of the present moment—an invaluable asset to a world in distress.

What Is This Self?   35

IT'S PRACTICE

The Chinese character *xing* (姓) conveys the nature of Zen practice; its meanings include "to walk," "to do," "to make a path," and "to act in concert with." Notice each of these meanings is a practical action lifted by the ceremony of paying close attention. Thich Nhat Hanh once described watching a mother brush her child's long hair as the moment when he finally understood that ritual is care, the quality of being deeply absorbed in doing something with no-thought and no-self. The long, slow movement of the brush; the gentle firmness with the knots; the complete concentration; the consecration of me and you approaching no "other." Love discovers itself in ceremonies of deep attention.

Same with zazen. The slow movements of breath and undivided awareness (with no "I am concentrating" or "I am doing") consecrates the place where you are, and at the deepest level repays a kindness that is hard to name. This ritual offering of unqualified awareness is a state in which consciousness can naturally transform. It propitiates nothing and seeks no results. Instead, each thing is enlightened a little by your steady attention. Even difficulties, uncertainty, fear, and anguish are accepted, and in being so embraced they turn out to be not what you thought. Ninth-century poet Po Chu-I celebrates the wisdom that zazen enjoys as "thoughts begin where words end" and "sharing the mind that's forgotten mind." Sharing it with all that is, no barrier.

IT'S ATTENTION

The iconoclastic fifteenth-century Japanese monk and poet Ikkyu Sojun was also a master calligrapher. Somebody once seeking to own a treasured Ikkyu calligraphy asked him to inscribe "a distillation of the highest wisdom." Ikkyu promptly took up his brush and inscribed the Chinese character for *attention*.

The visitor was dissatisfied. "Is that all?"

If you've ever tried to pay the kind of attention zazen asks of us, you'll know "Is that all?" to be a ridiculous question. But Ikkyu obligingly took up his brush again and added two more characters to fully flesh out the matter: *attention, attention*.

"But what does attention mean?" the person asked, staring at *attention, attention, attention*.

So Ikkyu kindly laid the matter bare in just three more characters: *Attention means attention.*

Nothing gets past Ikkyu to be added to the matter of attention bare enough to distill the wisdom of emptiness. Any excursion of linear mind is refused as zazen over and over again returns us to our original self, which is unfrayed by picking and choosing. Essential reality and a bare "nothing but attention" cannot be separated. Zazen explores this continually; what opens is always just enough. And underlying this frugality is trust in the mind, trust in life, trust in your human right to be here and awake.

Perhaps we could say that zazen introspects on not making yourself up. *Shikantaza*, Dogen's Japanese translation of the Chinese term for "just sitting," is zazen matured into the act of firmly declining to manifest self in the offer of moment-by-moment bare awareness. This unmaking is not done with attention trained on any particular thing at all, but by a disciplined willingness to arrive moment-by-moment right where you are in the unadorned state of *being*.

The "just" In "just sitting" cannot be underestimated. Attention discovers the unending productions of the mind that populate the verbal soundtrack of our lives. No wonder the twentieth-century Tibetan Buddhist master Chögyam Trungpa called meditation "just one insult after another," acknowledging the shock of how relentlessly and subtly the mind can resist quietening down and healing into what is.

Declining the mind's offer of resistance without opposing it becomes a subtle, patient skill. When we offer ourselves in this way, we're neither important nor unimportant. And for anything rich, creative, and fresh to be born, this mind has to be available to us. The rest is just doing what we *think* we know.

Adding some special dream concept like *buddha* to Zen practice adds too much. Another Ikkyu calligraphy states, "That stone buddha deserves all the bird shit that it gets!" I think that makes the point. All suppositions, however wonderful, are extra to the already complete nature of what is.

Attending implies following closely with what is happening, not leading or controlling. In offering such attention, a readiness brims without any "getting ready." The notable contemporary koan master John Tarrant counters the forward rush of mind with a highly practical koan: "Quick! Don't get ready!" "Getting ready" hopes to get safely in front of the moment, thereby missing it completely. Be fast enough to quell that default twitch of the mind and you are presence, readiness itself.

Ikkyu's account of the inside of "attention, attention, attention" flows and opens the way attention does, the way reality does: "Flowers are silent . . . silence is silent . . . the mind is a silent flower . . . the the silent flower of the world opens."

By the end, you can't tell flower of mind from flower of world; flowering is all. Practicing zazen regularly, you begin to notice throughout your day the open moments of mind fallen eloquently silent: needing nothing, wanting nothing, each thing expressing the universe with its sheer presence. This sheer availability is always here when you notice that it is.

Ikkyu's "silent" is not no sound, though. Rather, "silent" is a one-word koan resolved as zazen. It's a silence of wanting, a silence of any impulse to move off, reject, or demand, a silence toward difference. And "silence is silent" has no opinions, no urge to arrange reality for the self. Zazen is a kind of gradual discovery of what this silent silence might be, how roomy things are when "the silent flower of the world" opens to you. Feel what your heart knows about this.

At every point, reality is exactly as awake as we are. When we're dead to the world, reality is exactly as dead to us. We can't fall out of its aliveness, but we can spend a lifetime with our backs turned toward it. Strange, I know.

AND IT'S REALITY

"Attention is reality and reality is attention," concluded Flora Courtois (1916–2000), the remarkable lay practitioner recognized by Maezumi Roshi (1931–1995) as independently enlightened prior to becoming a Zen student. It's as bare and plain as the moment of birth or the last moments of life, shorn of all self-concern, where every breath is your whole life—life and death undivided.

Attention is "the end of thinking your living," said Courtois. Not seeking something called "enlightenment," attention itself enlightens each moment, with each thing here in its own right, complete. "Reflect now whether any being or any world is left outside of the present moment," Dogen directs.

Such attention is not simple to master, yet it is already alive in you. Be guided by the countless stray moments in any given day in which, if you notice, the burden of self just slips off and you can be totally contented with the feeling of a pebble in your hand, the sound of water, the look of the sky, shadows moving in the light . . . The fullness of empty reality is always on offer. Only our negligence toward it can diminish us.

And in approaching the supposed impossibility of quieting the mind to "hear" the silence between thoughts, be buoyed by the spirit of the great English sculptor Henry Moore. Asked close to the end of his life whether there was a secret to life, he said yes, there is. "The secret to life is this: have something you devote your entire life to, something you bring your whole life to, every day." He added, "And the most important thing is, it must be something that you cannot possibly do."[1]

It is this productive tension with impossibility presented by the Zen koan that in the end gives us the fearlessness that steps forward and takes firm hold of the tiger's whiskers.

A WILLING CRISIS OF MIND

Self-consciousness fades in zazen to the degree that it is replaced by "Who is this?" Once called "me," now no longer in need of a name, and with nothing to brace against, wonder becomes your mind. This feeling of attention being finally met on its own ground is where the heart facing a world on fire can begin to transmute an anguished "What can I do?" into a recognition of how much we share in a wider mind that can perceive the entire field of possibilities. Perhaps it begins to speak in terms more like "What is wanted here?" or "What does this need me to see?"

Zen koans form an impasse for the thinking mind that, persisted with, can become the open, unobstructed way of no-mind, and all that it can know for itself. Koans don't loiter at the entrance, waiting for something special, or hang around in rarefied states of mind. They draw the intelligence of emptiness into the heart of earthy, everyday life, refining a practical reliance on not-knowing that subscribes to no dream of separation. They follow Dogen's *Instructions to the Cook* to "turn things, while being turned." They use the flow of what is happening as the means of propulsion, which means we always have what we need, and nothing is actually missing.

To take up a koan is to willingly accept enduring a crisis of mind that cannot be resolved by the usual means. The mind that has been trained to identify and establish difference as the basis of all meaning has to be healed back into the infinitely varied completeness of rivers, earth, wind, stars, and all other beings—a completeness confirmed throughout the entire mysterious being called "me."

Impasse can be a richly dark, groping kind of place, and koan mind learns to appreciate that darkening, to open a more dark-adapted eye. When a crisis can no longer be denied, life becomes more sharply real, and discoveries can break through the wall of what you thought you knew. It seems it is good for human beings to face impossible problems, to find how to accept the risk to your dignity, to see the impossible become the improbable and the improbable become your true self, simply and helpfully doing what seems most needed.

Crisis itself becomes koanlike when accepted as a question with the force to overturn the thinking that created it, to heal us back into a more viable reality. You can use koans to learn how to accede to the intensity of facing an impasse, and then, how impasse can abruptly turn into a wide field of benefaction.

And so koans leave minds on more intimate terms with reality, more at home in crisis, more willing to examine fear's claim that "I'm in here and it's out there" and instead offer "This too is me."

Koans will not engineer a better security. That would require that the crisis confronting and threatening us must lie outside ourselves, whereas the true refuge turns out to be just what is, which is continuous with what we are: there is no "outside" to this. The mind that koans wake up is not alarmed, but rather buoyed by the fluid, empty, passing-through status of all beings and things. The official final statement on ecological wholeness issued by the United Nations Conference on the Human Environment, held in Stockholm in 1972, which was precursor to the 1997 Kyoto Protocol, concurred:

Life holds to one central truth: that all matter and energy needed for life moves in great closed circles from which nothing escapes and to which only the driving fire of the sun is added. . . . Of all that there is on earth, nothing is taken away by life, and nothing is added by life—but nearly everything is used by life, used and re-used in thousands of complex ways, moved through vast chains of plants and animals and back again to the beginning.[2]

The interbeing so explicitly described here, which must inform and guide deep adaptation to the climate crisis if we are to find a productive field of continuing emergence—that is, one closely aligned with the very nature of ecological reality—is fundamental to the Zen koan.

PLAINSPOKEN, PLAIN AS DAY

Koans are drawn from live encounters in which plain, unglorified words are spoken, and questions responded to from the ground of undivided reality. These words and responses are irreconcilable with logic but fully reconcilable with experience. To work with a koan—better yet, to let it work with you—is to be tipped out of the discursive mind and back onto the original, empty ground. When you see into a koan it is said that you see with the same eyes and share the same mind as the one who spoke those left-of-field words some thousand or so years ago. Not explicated, not elaborated, not offered in immense and dazzling sutras, these plain words just refuse the way minds expect to work. They are spoken not from some sanctuary of carefully constructed peace, but from a calm that is wrought right within the rough and tumble of ordinary and sometimes severely difficult conditions in life.

Emptiness sees us right through time—our body, our aging, and even our possible extinction. It cuts clear through to the sky to perceive birds flying, mist dissolving, and all that is pouring toward and through us whenever we're not locked inside the dream of the separate self. And it's entirely ordinary.

ORDINARY

As noted in the introduction, it was during chaotic times of war, disease, and sociopolitical collapse in eighth-century China that koan mind initially stirred so boldly into life, ready to help. Koans appeared as medicine—immediate, earthy, practical means of recovering coherence, steadiness, buoyancy, capacity, and endurance in a time of overwhelming disruption.

Their earthiness derives from the premodern Daoist cast of mind, which long predated Buddhism in China and was the stream that Buddhism joined to become Chan, the originating tradition of Zen. The Chinese character rendered as "meaning," for example, holds thoughts and feelings as inextricable from wild nature, locating mind seamlessly in the entirely natural world. There is nowhere else. The Dao has no "outside."

As Buddhism slowly trickled north and east from the South Asian subcontinent, complex, abstract Sanskrit sutras were rendered into earthy, concrete, ideographic Chinese, opening up a richly poetic and metaphoric expressive power of awakened mind in the process. For example, the character corresponding to the word *universe* in Chinese uncoils into "the mountains, rivers, the great, wide Earth, the sun, the moon, and the stars." This very mortal body; everyday things themselves; creatures; elements like fire, water, earth, wind, and wood; as well as bones, bone marrow, leaves, shadows, qualities of light, dragons, hungry ghosts, the sun, the moon, and the stars—all are welcome to the play of manifesting buddhamind.

When a very young Zhaozhou came to his teacher, Nanquan, asking, "What is the Dao?" Nanquan told him, "Ordinary mind is the Dao." When Zhaozhou asked how or indeed whether to try to direct himself toward this wonder, Nanquan explained that if you turn toward it, it turns away from you. To direct yourself toward it is to turn it away.

Trying to take hold with the knowing mind can only leave you more remote from what is vast and boundless and is actually looking through your very own eyes. Discover how to let it approach and seize you, then ordinary things reveal it plain as day. It's a wild and spontaneous reality, the one we're in! We have to meet it just that way.

Arguably, the essence and spirit imparted by the entire Buddhist canon arrives in the spontaneous gestures, deeds, poetry, laughter, and humor of the Chan masters. The *wu wei* sense of not-doing, which contemporary writer and translator David Hinton renders as selfless, spontaneous, even wild, is alive in the playful, improvisatory spirit of encounters that became valued as "public cases" of awake mind. By analogy with case law, koans stand as publicly witnessed and attested precedents that ring with publicly tested and confirmed authority all the way down to today, each holding open the chance to test and find yourself there, more awake. Why? Because each koan openly reveals the fire of the absolute ablaze in the most ordinary details of the relative world.

Ryokan was an endearing and beloved eighteenth-century Japanese mendicant monk, calligraphic artist, and poet. In wonderful celebrations of serious lunacy he made his unorthodox nature clear to anyone who cared to look. At the height of one summer, he announced to local villagers, "Today I will air the entire Buddhist canon in the Five Scoop Hut! Please come and see." "Airing the canon" is the traditional practice of setting out a temple's complete set of Buddhist classics and flipping through the pages to help them dry out and for the merit it's thought to generate.

This was an amazing offer. Millions of words, tens of thousands of pages! How would Ryokan air the entire canon in his tiny house? The villagers duly made their way to Ryokan's hut as instructed, but there were no books of the holy canon on display at all. Only Ryokan, lying naked. On his drumlike belly was written the phrase, "entire canon." The villagers were dumbfounded. Of course, finding you have no words can be an excellent sign that a koan has begun to take you seriously. Ryokan made himself a "public case," a living koan, knowing very well that all koans are live fragments of one story, one epic, one mind, one masterpiece.

Ordinary is alight with presence, fire, life. With close, mindful attention, nothing is ordinary; the natural poetry of the world finds its intensity in each thing just as it is. Every breaking wave confirms the nature of this universe; the life of stars appears in every dandelion, the mystery of cause and effect is evident and mysterious in the shifting shadows of leaves stirred by the breeze, pooling and vanishing into one another.

THE OPEN HUMAN HAND

Working and living with koans is not a matter of taking them up as holy writ, or like genuflecting before a saint. The Zen masters of old, like the historic Buddha, were ordinary human beings who determined to open themselves up to seamless reality, and then to requite that blessing by holding themselves open to the questions, efforts, and bafflement of others, all in service of their inborn desire to wake up. These irascible ancestors follow no expected script. They come around the corner of your mind to collide with you before you can get ready to hold them at bay. Your job is to get past yourself enough to rise directly and equally to seize the moment of this encounter.

If you were to ask them how they knew to say what they said, there'd only be generous laughter or a pregnant silence for you to gestate in. Their "method" has no name. If you were to inquire, "Why speak these plain yet very difficult words," their response might be as simple as, "It is important to touch things and reach beings."

Every being counts. Every human being a matter of infinite value.

Consider the splayed human hand, dipped in ochre or paint and pressed against any firm surface—cave wall, church wall, school wall, rock wall. Australian rock art sites overflow with these signature greetings. Each one is a heart's claim in the present tense: I am. Here. Even when a million years old, "here!" and more intimately, "I am," it still insists. Its "here" is timeless.

You can fit your own hand in the handprint of someone who lived 63,000 years ago. A perfect fit. The same no-time exactly in each handprint.

And the humanness of these images is not shy. Within the enduring pattern of five phalanges repeating throughout the vertebrate kingdom, only among the hominids is one phalange fully opposable to the other four: the short but proud thumb, muscular base of all the spectacular human manipulations of this Earth that are now visible even from space.

Another thing about this universal hand mark: it is splayed, presented at full stretch. Like the Chinese character for fire at the beginning of each chapter of this book, it is radiant, reaching out from its singular base to establish the eternally mysterious space of just where it is. It confirms presence while not engaged or proclaimed in directing or manipulating anything at all. It is empty-handed presence.

Now try examining your own hand that is not splayed, but with fingers and thumb lined up and the wrist turned in a sideways, linear view. The lively Australian indigenous thinker Tyson Yunkaporta suggests this image to describe the directed flow or push of discursive, expository, literate thought—in other words, this leads to that, this causes that, this begins here and ends there, declaiming this belongs here, that doesn't belong here . . .[3] This linear hand places us in linear time, a teleological universe and mind, a persuasive or even coercive, categorical knowing. This sideways handprint shows up on no walls, but deeply writes itself into every human mind schooled in written literacy.

The open hand has no such beginning or end implied. It's alive at all times and allows every part to equally suggest the whole. In the same way that every flickering flame of fire is equally and wholly fire, every joint, fingerprint, planes of the palm, and exclamation mark of thumb equally and wholly makes the direct contact called "Here!" "Now!" "Human!"

This hand and mind is open, empty, unarmed, receptive. Like a field of grass, rocks, tiny flowers, wind ripples, water ripples, bird squawks, and shadows, the hand is a field of infinite possibility, utterly human, telling the astonishing singular story of this universe in every detail: "I am," beyond where thought or time can capture. And yet this hand is all-too-humanly able, in the story of this world, to take, grab, and harm, which is why laws evolve in recognition of this, to keep the overreaching human being in hand.

And every part of such a hand or mind says or sings the whole field, the whole hand, the whole being. Like a hologram, every particle holds the whole and reveals one radiant fire of emptiness. As Hongzhi (1091–1157) puts it:

> Seeing existence without considering it existent;
> Turning the hand over and back

Consider your own hand once more. Turn the hand over: emptiness, absence of any "thing." Now turn the hand back: form, presence, fingerprints, never to be seen in this universe again.

One hand, like everything in this universe, not two—only *this*, far beyond all ideas of existent and nonexistent.

Is anything left out of this hand? Can it possibly be here without all that is here?

PALM-OF-THE-HAND STORIES

Koans are small enough to fit in the palm of your hand—short, sharp, memorable keys to the doors by which we close ourselves off from direct contact with reality. Koans undo the ways we make ourselves up. Coming as stories, they contain their seeds of transformation encased in a burr. Seeds are psychologically chaste and compact, pointed so as to burrow deep into the earth and lodge there, able to unfurl their meaning and give rise to shoots, saplings, and great trees that can shelter a whole community. They are also able to lie inert for vast periods of time and still hold their nourishment, their viability.

And yet, also subtly hooked, they attach to us and come with us whether we like it or not, whether we understand them or not, until they sprout in their own good time, our own good time. Stories, like seeds, are the most ancient human mnemonic and oral form of literacy. They recall us to what we most hold dear, are beautifully hard to shake from memory, and carry the fullness of mysteries in discrete, portable forms that come with us even when the mystery has not yet broken through in us.

Koans are the splayed, empty hand using words that encase the liberating seed of nonlinear mind. Having a seedlike quality, they lodge in the mind and are known by heart just as poems are known, and as such they continue to resonate and break open. Each koan brings the bare essence of the Dharma, the endlessly productive and creative tension between undivided, formless reality and tender, poignant, mortal life, which ripens into the true nature of this self.

The subtle joy of Zen mind lies in its willingness to include and be with what is, in its daring to stand not one inch off from where we are now. When you offer to whatever appears—wind roar, birdcall, floor creak, dismayed face, tinge of sorrow, edge of fear—an unqualified "You are welcome here," you find yourself welcomed here, your poignant, pungent humanity welcomed by this tender, watchful Earth. Any story worth remembering confirms this.

Our pain for the world and our power to take part in the healing of the Earth come from the same place. Each breath is the Earth breathing. Awakenings and realizations come by nature. Don't strain to get there, as there has never been a "somewhere" to go to. To offer yourself over and over again to the question "Who is this? What is this?" rather than to the answer, where your safety seems invested, is not to try for an outcome. It is to offer yourself.

Zen koan practice is a kind of transforming ceremony of awareness. It can include, when it likes to, a touch of brilliant lunacy to restore us in a form that is more tender, crazy, human, and humorous, more one with the whole Earth. It carries the wise lunacy of becoming willing to make our tenacious sense of an isolated self a little more precarious, to place it in productive crisis, to not know in order to catch sight of all that is emergent and yet to be realized in the current emergency—what a way to open to the way!

That open human hand brings nothing with it, seeks to touch *what is* in person, to receive and bestow the direct impression of reality. It reaches, touches, but does not grasp. It is a warm, entirely human hand, a greeting, an edgeless field of emergent meaning, a network of touch. And a network is a fire, a free exchange of being.

Consider the crazed lines in the palm of your hand. Compare them to the crazed and sinuous pathways of water across the land, pathways shaped by resistance in the act of yielding. It is a kind of fire, these networks of secret flow, through the land, the hand, through hands that touch and join together, the form of love this interbeing ignites. That upright, open hand has some intimation of "Stop!" "Notice!" "See!" in its radiant gesture. But that is right there along with the greeting "Welcome!"

There is no way to "save the Earth," which is already complete in every moment when we see clearly. That being so, each measured response that has immediate sympathetic resonance with this fact and reaches out from there is as much "saving the Earth" as anything else. This is the way of crisis opening us to ourselves.

Each of us is in the act of finding all of us—our shared awareness, actions, words, thoughts, gifts, and dreams. Turning things around while turning with the flowing world, we form one field of fire, ignited by the deep courtesy of paying attention. It is this form of loving attention that reclaims your existence in the physical world, restores its mystery, and lets the Earth begin to think along with you.

CODA: THE TIGER'S KINDNESS

Awakening to what is,
now we must defend the Earth
from ourselves
with a fierce love.

—RAFAEL JESÚS GONZÁLEZ

Where does this fierce love hide? An old Korean koan secretes an intent to defend the Earth that is fierce and loving enough to bring us face to face with the mystery of ourselves: "The tiger fears the human heart. The human fears the tiger's kindness."

As a child I made regular pilgrimages to an oddly dark corner of the natural history museum. In a glass case, among other moldy specimens of taxidermy, was a diminutive tree shrew clinging to a desiccated twig, staring from the gloom with huge nocturnal eyes of wonder, or terror. A handwritten card simply said, "Our Earliest Ancestor." This tiny, frail mammal from which hominids eventually derive and branch was already darting for cover in the time of dinosaurs and saber-toothed tigers. As apex predators, tigers are paradoxically among the most vulnerable of animals, yet how large they loom in the minds of the apex predator we humans have now become. Does our ancestral memory include seven-inch teeth buried deep in the back of our fragile necks?

The natural world bears the cost of how hard we strain to live "safely" short of a full admission of mortality, letting that denial strangle basic human kindness and joy. What potent, transforming heart energy can live pinned down by primal, unapproachable fear? Fear battles with a wonder that is close to envy as we descendants of a tiny tree shrew stare into fathomless tiger eyes.

"The tiger fears the human heart." We are born in a world that finds it unquestionably correct to "fix" nature and "improve" its course from a strictly human point of view, calling it progress while turning a cold heart toward the fate of every nonhuman being in our vicinity that is not a pet or source of food, recreation, or wealth. The tiger's fear of a fear-shrunken human heart is unsurprising; there's little room for kindness in it.

At the same time, the tiger imprints its fiery beauty and relaxed self-containment on our imagination, and in this way the tiger also makes us more human. Within the tiger's magnetic pull is the covert recognition of how much its creaturely excellence is shaped by its capacity to endure great difficulty and skill in securing food, as well as to survive our dangerous human presence. To the tiger's burden of recreational trophy hunters we've recently added deforestation, habitat destruction, and the perverse commodification of tigers in order to harvest their skins, penises, and teeth.

But next we learn with a jolt that "the human fears the tiger's kindness."

To truly glimpse the tiger's kindness is to awaken with a roar from the dream of a separate self and cease hiding the full capacity of our hearts from ourselves, for it is the sting of mortality that opens the gift of life. The tiger's kindness lays bare how a natural tenderness toward the living Earth and all her beings is cauterized by our unwillingness to suffer our awareness of mortality right to its radiant core. Our fear of death drains life from the Earth.

The kindness of the tiger raises Yunmen's question—"Then what is this self?"—into the light of our death. This is a question poised to take everything away and give you back your heart and mind at ease in impermanence, relaxed and alert in recognizing the whole Earth and all its creatures as not other than this mysterious self—the whole Earth as medicine.

Tolerance of the inevitability of death, which is final proof of the impermanence and uncertainty of all conditions, lies at the foundation of fierce love. A Zen student of mine once offered these deeply relaxed words to me just days away from his death: "The beauty of our life arises out of that very unreliability of all our conditions: that nothing is certain, luckily!"

His "luckily" sees far into the kindness of the tiger, where all things take their ease and find their perfect fit. How suddenly small it feels to scramble after a security that cannot exist in the grandeur of a universe where everything, including the universe itself, is alight with the fire that runs through all things.

A shockingly narrow and deluded human sense of self predates the entire living Earth. In exactly the same move, our small, unworthy forms of fear severely predate our own reserves of love. The kindness of the tiger lays bare the true face of love and how perverse it is to hide from it.

In our precarious shared moments on Earth right now, doing anything less than paying keen attention is not an option. Not-knowing uses the all-embracing no-fear that is the ultimate kindness of the tiger. "Completely using life, we cannot be held back by life. Completely using death, we cannot be held back by death," says Dogen, explaining in full the tiger's kindness.

Waking up reaches for us with exactly the same strength of our long-ing to be fully here, in complete reunion with what is, fierce as tiger.

not just about me
suddenly the blue
in his eyes

火

2

PRECARIOUS

Benefit what cannot be benefitted; do what cannot be done.

—GREAT MASTER MAZU

Celebrate your lunacy, pray for help!

—TIBETAN LOJONG SLOGAN

Apart from a cry of "Fire!" the shortest human prayer torn from the throat of emergency on a rapidly heating Earth is "Help!" Meanwhile, the everyday common prayer—the only one we ever really need, despite its relative absence from our lips and hearts—is simply "Thank you."

For it is amazing to be, to be here at all.

But moving beyond just the human, the singular, silent cry of life on Earth right now is "Precarious!" This too is closer to a prayer than it may seem; it's an honest, vulnerable, lucid confession of alarm. This admission of vulnerability is itself a search for the strong nerve of resilience.

OVER THE HILL AND INTO THE DARK

The times are always uncertain until we cease longing for certainty, and only then do they become truly interesting. The planetary crisis we're in together is now simply the given—the strange, inarguable gift of what is. The fervent half-prayer of "Precarious!" overhears the realization that any escape is futile. Who now in good faith can dispute planetary heating and its appalling consequences and our drift toward civilizational suicide, ruined lands, biodiversity collapse, record-breaking megafires and megafloods, and new pandemics. And then there's our shadow pandemic, too: panic, confusion, and conspiratorial rage, shadowed by dread, anxiety, and depression.

The Industrialized West has metastasized into almost every corner of this living planet with a turbocharged drive to extract wealth at all cost to life, the hell-bent intent that has now been normalized by democracies and tyrannies alike. The momentum of living by damage has slipped beyond our reckoning and control. Our fractious geopolitical world is now mirrored by massive geophysical changes, as the weather and Earth herself turns angry.

Meanwhile, social media has as much fractured as formed the basis for a consensual, factually based understanding from which to engage the huge questions. Conspiracy, paranoia, misinformation, organized disinformation, and contempt for evidence undermine a coherent response. First the pandemic and now war stalks the world again. Where's the center that will hold, the sure place in which to invest trust?

It's impossible to avert your eyes, difficult to see how to respond, and impossible not to long to do so. Even listing the ways in which "so much is wrong" begins to feel like a verbal *totentanz*, as in the old medieval woodcuts depicting the dance of death: heavy-laden words joining hands with the skeletal grim reaper, dancing us over a hill of doom into the dark.

The planetary dangers that haunt us make our time an exquisite moment, piercing and inescapable. Also baffling to the point of provoking fresh realizations, hence the description of this time as a "gift" brimming with untested possibilities right along with potentially dire consequences. Dare we celebrate the way it stretches us, this strange privilege of being alive right now? Can we embrace the sheer lunacy of our moment, in which the biggest human "ask" in history up to now has chosen us?

A koan scandalizes all suppositions (literal, rational, empirical, neurotic) that hold up the shaky sky of human knowing and fearing, until the leaves blowing in the street, the wave welling over a rock, the eyelashes of the cow all share the same realm as this mind. The shock of this can stoke new depths of fiery, fiercely protective love for the Earth. With luck, this love is fierce enough to protect our home from the worst impulses in ourselves and turn them to good.

DARKENING THIS MIND

Luckily there's another, very different kind of darkness—that of the mind relaxing in a state of active not-knowing. In this fertile darkness, the search for how to respond can grow more surefooted, agile, and in sync with events rather than pitted against them. Not-knowing is like leaning back against the tree that is always there, older than any forest; or as Dogen puts it, taking "the backward step that turns your light inward to illuminate yourself." Not-knowing introspection and self-inquiry—as in "What is this self?"—moves us into intimacy with who this is and what is happening.

The ecocrisis of our time raises the question of the true nature of our human presence on the Earth as a koan that rightly exerts an almost overwhelming pressure on our hearts. It cannot be resolved, and the suffering it causes cannot be relieved without breaking through the paradigm that is so relentlessly causing it. Zen koans help us grow skilled in tolerating a precarious state of mind, and not turning away but growing curious instead. That we can't go forward in the usual way becomes the strangely valuable offer of the moment. Not-knowing, in the spirit of improvisation, accepts all offers! And the Zen koan turns every obstacle into the way.

Take a despairing reaction like "There is nothing I can do to stop this disaster!" Looking beyond the ideas of "I," and "stop," and even the activity of "doing," can we even dare to look deeply into the crisis and not-know what it is, or that it is so? Perhaps even disaster loses its power of impasse when scrutinized by a trusting form of productive doubt. Can something be done with less *doing*, using the calm inside the moments that can be created within an emergency when what is happening is met with not-knowing?

Or consider the desperate sense of "This is beyond me!" Aha! Yes, it is! Reality is definitely beyond the claim of "me." Might it be possible to live tragically aware of the immensity of what we face and yet rely on the ground of fundamental joy that dares to meet fear? Not-knowing meets and disables fear and can discern more clearly how a situation is moving and what is needed right in the midst of the unfolding moment.

The way we have framed reality is plainly out of kilter and out of date. Koan mind breaks the rigid frame and makes an ally out of uncertainty, asking it to be our guide in the darkness.

CRISES SECRETE THEIR OWN HEALING

Every koan has a bit of the apocalyptic about it, lifting the veil that this dream of a separate self throws over the wholeness of reality. *Apocalypse* implies destruction of a world, but hiding in that word is the older meaning, that of a necessary revelation, a veil torn away, leaving no choice but to see what is hidden from us in plain sight.

Similarly, people speak of a healing crisis in the course of an illness, a looked-for climax poised to tip us either toward death or toward the dawn of healing. "Medicine and sickness heal each other": Yunmen is pointing to suffering healing into nondual awakening, the dream of separation waking into the reality of no "other." Precarious emotional states likewise can intensify into a healing crisis in which seemingly indigestible anger, fear, or grief can suddenly tip over and metabolize a general amnesty. That beautiful word *forgiveness* suggests the germination of ease within precariousness.

Crises shape and transform us all our lives. The limitations that grow apparent to a crawling infant become the seeming unlikelihood of learning to walk. Impasse is the unavoidable opportunity to see beyond expectations, suppositions, and impossibilities as they crumble before our eyes. Crisis, whether at the vast or intimately personal level, is what reveals that there is no "normal," despite all strenuous efforts to coax one into being. Not-knowing is relaxing into trusting this.

FIRST RESPONDER

There once was a captain of a racing yacht that had completely turtled, then rerighted itself twice in the vast, twenty-meter waves of a storm that also snapped the mast. His panicked crew of five shouted maddened suggestions at one another in the roaring wind and waves. The captain later reported that in the very midst of the terrifying chaos, he "took a moment to make a few notes" to determine their position, the wind, and the wave direction. He was calculating the one safe path to a possible port. His calm focus and discernible lack of panic helped settle the crew. They grew quiet and alert, and against very steep odds, crewed the stricken vessel to safe harbor.

Koan-honed mind can be just like finding the energy and even-minded awareness of the first responder in an emergency. It rouses awareness in a way not unlike the philosopher José Ortega y Gasset's mind of a hunter, alive to all points in the widest possible field of attention: "The hunter knows that he does not know what is going to happen. . . . Thus he needs to prepare an attention which does not consist in riveting itself on the presumed, but consists precisely in not presuming anything and in avoiding inattentiveness . . . a 'universal' attention, which does not inscribe itself at any point and tries to be on all points."[1]

All points are equal in such a field of alert attention. When you allow yourself to breathe and slow down in zazen, you inhabit time more bodily and fully and gradually cease the effort of manufacturing yourself. You spare yourself, the way meditation spares you. Then Mazu's challenging koan, "Benefit what cannot be benefitted, do what cannot be done," begins to make real sense. There is no heroic injunction here to do the impossible. When you are more seamlessly spare and complete with just where you are, there is little or no doing at all. Then what needs doing is already getting done, before any knowing.

There's no rush possible here, and nowhere to get to. You cannot love, sit in meditation, or live with a koan speedily. "Too fast, too forceful, you miss the way," as the Buddha advised. Not-knowing inhabits time and place too fully for that.

A friend described taking a long walk on a beach in Australia one day during a prolonged drought and meeting an indigenous man gathering pippies, delicately purple, butterfly-winged shell creatures that burrow down in the wet sand on the edge of the waves. He was finding them as if by magic, as though he'd read the tide and the wind and the sky and the curve of the beach exactly right. My friend fell into conversation with him and learned where the fish were running, and that they'd gone way upriver and were not coming down.

Interesting, she reflected, as her suppositions went to the drought, the saltwater penetrating far up into the freshwater reaches of the river. She volunteered these busy thoughts, then slowed down enough to notice. "Ah, but why aren't they coming down?" she finally asked him. Dropping a few more pippies into his bucket, he looked at her as if she were strange. After a while, giving her time to pull out of herself recognition of the deeper way of things, he at last gently said, "They don't *want* to."

There is a pushiness that characterizes the attitude of seeing the world as something to stand over and control rather than sense and move in accord with its natural unfolding. That attitude will ultimately fail, for it completely misses the agency, the self-mastery, and the utter right to be here that all living things possess. It misses the ebb and flow of what you might call the Dao, which is beyond any "doing"—like the wind that blows or the water that flows as it will. We have no way out of this, fortunately.

For such wisdom to dawn for my friend, to help her arrive where she truly was, she first had to willingly endure the indignity of uncertainty. She had to relinquish knowing in order to become aware of something lying outside of knowing's reach. She had to be willing to lose in order to receive. As with every koan, knowing has to come undone.

NOT-KNOWING IS WILLING VULNERABILITY

In confirming the fire that runs through all things, every koan touches something thoroughly at rest at the heart of our precariousness. Lunacy and prayer are celebrated as they arrive together in the process of waking up. To celebrate your lunacy *is* to pray for help, which blesses your original lunacy—one great and round risk, sharply worth taking.

Lojong is the Tibetan practice of working with provocative slogans in order to train in compassion. The slogan given as an epigraph at the start of this chapter brings sly, subversive spirit to the tender process of awakening: "Celebrate your lunacy!" Start where you are and raise it to strong awareness! And then the slogan immediately hinges that risk with an equally wise and emphatic admonition to "pray for help!" Such a risk is fruitful; precariousness and resilience discover each other, they inter-are. To choose uncertainty (a strange gift!) is to open your hands to loss all the way down to your personal mortality. It's the choice to allow the sorrow of lost expectations. There's great tenderness in this choice. It hurts, but acceptance of such hurt creates and enlarges resilience.

Every Zen koan, in responding to that universal prayer for help, takes a thorough sounding of the lunacy of being human. This is plain in the dynamic of a teacher-student encounter, that shared improvisation of awakening at the heart of Zen. What student and teacher handle together is so very plain, it takes so long to see; it requires sharp moments of surprise, rugs pulled out from under you, laughter and play, and shared tears. Our fundamental lunacy—that nothing is hidden except in plain sight— is turned around into what opens the mind. And the prayer for help initiates it with the yearning to wake up and break free of your wonderfully thorough self-binding.

When a monk asked Zhaozhou, "What is my teacher?" Zhaozhou rendered himself, and in the same breath, all teachings, completely transparent: "Clouds rising out of mountains, streams entering valleys without a sound." It is also papers blowing down a street, the screak of a door hinge, the faded blue of that old desk. It's you when you can find nothing to stand on and no place to fall.

There's a valuable lunacy in choosing not to move off from the danger of failing to know how to respond to a koan, and accepting the struggle to become a little more fearless, and then to observe how that fearlessness turns the failure to know into not-knowing, which in turn can find nothing that is in the way, nothing that is not the way.

Ever so gracefully, Zhaozhou also lightly evokes how formless is form: momentary clouds rising as the solidity of the mountain, the busy stream pouring into valleys, soundless at the source of all thought. Form, emptiness—who can finally tell them apart? The one who cannot is the constant, patient guide.

It's *you*, when you can find nothing to stand on and no place to fall.

POETRY, KOAN, PRAYER

Koan encounters are made out of awakening, words, and silence.

Koan, like poetry, likes language prepared to be mercifully hard on itself. Koan language cares deeply enough to be unsentimental—wasting nothing, mimicking nothing, never deceiving. This is language that touches inarguable reality. Realization speaks no explanatory prose and slips free as fire from attempts to capture it. Where prose has a linear, hopeful longing for knowing and persuading, poetry depends on the not-knowing that lands us where we can know it for ourselves. Poetry does best in the direct and ordinary language—of ants, stones, twigs, dust, blood, fear, pain, love—which is also the language of the absolute.

In this way, poetry and koan both share something close to prayer within the precariousness of being human. If you look deeply, the Earth lives in us as a poem, a prayer, and now as a koan. Koans are not needed to complete the winging bird or the dissolving cloud. But they do let emptiness see into us and make brilliant use of our precariousness. Not-knowing is a kind of steady prayer for wholeness in the face of difficulty.

It is not so strange then that the word *precarious*, as derived from its Latin and Indo-European roots, means "questioning," "petitioning," and "prayer." The Latin root *precarius*, meaning "given as a favor, depending on the pleasure or mercy of others, of questionable force or permanence, uncertain," and *prex*, Latin for "prayer," as well as its earliest Indo-European root, *prek*, also meaning "prayer," brings the sense of an innate dependence on something beyond the self welling over into a plea for safety under pressure of disaster. The etymology of this word speaks to that visceral cry of the heart as you teeter high on a ladder. Precariousness is thus a prayer for help, just as crisis is an invitation to venture beyond the self into all that is actually here, ripe, in latent form.

The profound Buddhist teaching on the concept of the dependent co-arising of all things and all beings rests in this exacting nature of precariousness. We depend on one another. We arise together. We share the same no-ground. We manifest impermanence, all passing through one another and together. And this miracle of dependent co-arising manifests as the great flowering of life on Earth, which is now enduring one of its most bitter seasons.

Coming home takes place in uncertainty, even by means of uncertainty. The times are always uncertain until we cease longing for certainty, and then they become truly interesting. The beautiful lunacy of not-knowing, of relying on uncertainty, is an act of faith in what is, minus all the bargaining. Can you hear the prayer in that? The sober recognition that we are slipping into an ever more dangerous place may be the first time on Earth such a feeling can be said to be universal, nudging every single human being, making the very word *Earth* into a prayer on the breath.

Sustain the absorbed mental stillness of not-knowing, and this bubble of a human heart can break into river, flowing rocks, and flame.

WELCOME IT

A monk came to Zhaozhou, asking, "When times of great difficulty come to visit us, how should we meet them?" Zhaozhou replied, "Welcome."

Welcome is that vulnerable resilience speaking and listening, being curious and willing to meet precariousness and the fear it may arouse. The infinitely riskier choice is to live oblivious to what is happening, clinging to groundless expectations and living in conjecture. *Welcome* does not instruct us in how to act in a crisis; it just says to dare to directly greet what is. It takes the part of the timeless host that welcomes us as brief guests of the Earth, ready to offer some help.

This welcoming mind shares the fire of emptiness that runs through all things. It's the radical acceptance that turns the oncoming rush of circumstances into the way through. "You are welcome here" holds even painful states equal and unobjectionable. Roof creaking, birdcall, warmth, the weight of your body, the energy in your hands, the rising and falling breath—each thing is evenly welcomed.

Thus, you are welcomed exactly as you welcome, making the wonderfully reckless move that is our sole refuge in every time and place. Welcome sidesteps *difficult* and discovers something more interesting than fear.

All that has delivered us here just as we are—heart beating with our memories, dreams, hopes, and sorrows; kind and unkind thoughts and actions; loving and hateful moments; being equally ravished and dismayed by the beauty and fragility of the Earth—all of it is accepted as the emergent field within this difficult time. As the tenth-century Zen master Fayan Wenyi dared to say, "Right now there is nothing to reject." In Fayan's timeless "right now," all directions are open, and all things are blameless. We stumble to catch up with what is happening in each brief moment of the present, but luckily it can never go away.

MOST INTIMATE

Not-knowing shares with the most simple and ordinary things the mind that's forgotten mind: gray kangaroos lifting their faces in the paddock; the afternoon warmth remaining in the stone wall; an early cricket making the grass chirp; the steam rising from a mug of tea. So simply good. There is no end to it. As John Tarrant once put it, "When knowing stops, when thoughts about who we are fall away, vast space opens up and love appears."

Dizang let his student Fayan in on this open secret when he found him coming back through the monastery gates. He asked Fayan, "Where have you been?" and Fayan could only say in wonderment, "I have been wandering at random." Unfettered feet, not-knowing mind, curiously at ease. You can come back from a walk like this, having let trees and the wind take care of things.

Perceiving something beginning to drop away in Fayan, Dizang gently investigates: "What do you think of wandering?"

Fayan can say only, "I don't know." Sharing the mind that's forgotten mind, such not-knowing is a very ripe state, far from dreaminess or wooliness.

Dizang's next words bring him home through the gate completely: "Not-knowing is most intimate."

Fayan's body and mind dropped away with those words, like fruit heavy with ripeness.

The intimacy of not-knowing that can be honed in koan practice offers itself to the profound uncertainty of our moment.

Working with a koan teaches you how to come up to the barrier of difficulty again and again with nonjudging curiosity and unqualified interest, alert and undazzled, attending closely to what is happening. When you reach for that mind in crisis, the crisis becomes a koan, a matter to be valuably resolved. Then nonlinear mind can open a surprising way through that does not depend on what we think we know, but comes around the corner, moving crabwise, breaking free of expectations; it seeks to be congruent, not imposed.

Notice Fayan's "wandering at random" has no hint of straining for anything. Dreaming nothing up, but instead letting reality dream him up a little, he falls creatively open in all directions and fundamentally at ease, not suffering ideas about how things should, would, or could have been. Happy, lucky fool, enjoying just what is happening. *Happ*, the Old German root of the words *happening* and *happy*, means "luck." "Wandering at random" is lending yourself to the current and hedging no bets. It's like bodysurfing, where you entrust yourself to the brimming uncertainty of the wave, letting body become wave.

THE LUCK OF THE DAO

The soundest intuitions and clearest actions in response to the profound threat of ecological disaster begin in just such a state of fully conceding to what is and to just what we are. We agree to move with the deep movement of the Dao, and from there actions arise as gracefully and timely as grass bending in the wind or seeds broadcasting through the air.

For example, the flooding turbocharged by accelerating global warming is now becoming the most common natural disaster on the planet, especially in cities, with their vast hardened surfaces and narrow choke points of water flow. In response, the idea of "sponge cities" is emerging—restoring or creating gray-water wetlands that can absorb and slow water flow while also purifying the water as it flows overland. Another idea is to restore hardened stormwater canals back to their original soft creekbeds and rewilding earthen banks, which also returns these respite areas to wildlife in urban settings.

Leaning even further into the Dao is the idea of giving rivers the room they need to flood safely by protecting floodplain wetlands, reinstating ancient river channels, retaining and enhancing buffer strips along river frontages, and designing housing anchored in place on the ground but able to rise with floodwater and float safely in place. Moving in accord with the deep ideas of the Earth.

Another kind of example: A man was standing close to the head of a long queue of people waiting to get help with their cell phones. The woman in front of him being helped was having trouble communicating her needs and misunderstood what was being said about SIM cards. He gradually realized that she was a newly arrived Ukrainian war refugee with limited English. The noise of exasperation began to grow behind him as her difficulties dragged on. He could feel the air turning hostile. What could he do? The merest thing: although aware that she did not understand the complaining comments, he found himself instinctively just very slightly turning his body so that it shielded her, just enough to deflect the anger coming from the people in line so that it could pass harmlessly into himself and not beyond. Moving in accord with the deep idea of saving beings.

Not-knowing is the fertile, co-creative uncertainty that accords most closely with our unimaginable lives. Why unimaginable? Try to trace the causes of just one single thing—one moment, one breath, one grain of sand, one self. An infinitude of causes and effects fans out and out, with no beginning or end. This is a marvelous matter, a vast endowment landing entirely on its feet, exactly in you in every moment. This is what lights up plainly in realization and, luckily, is found in every moment. Unimaginable, this sheer existence. Human beings are astonishing.

Dizang's "Not-knowing is most intimate" resounds throughout this book. The conversation of those two, Dizang and Fayan, in the lengthening shadows of emptiness, is a glimpse at how thoroughly every teacher-student relationship—indeed, any two beings vulnerably open to each other's presence—is one instinctive, mutual improvisation in awakening. It is not-knowing in its most intimate state. The mysterious affinity that pervades the whole universe now is in play.

To be in such accord is a wonderful form of recklessness.

PRACTICE THIS

Years later, as a great teacher himself, Fayan was asked, "What is Buddha?" The old opening question once again: what is awakening and please tell me how to get it. Fayan responded with all the instructions ever needed for easing into a greater wakefulness: "First, I want you to practice it. Second, I want you to practice it."

It will never stop opening as long as you never do. A patient, willing darkening of the expectant mind becomes a skill—one that uncovers what lies silently beneath all surface agitation and fear, all appearances, all assumptions. It is something older, better, dearer, and more intimate than anything we could dream up.

And strangely familiar. After all, you subside into it effortlessly, body and mind, every time you yield to sleep. Any generous laughter or cry of joy shouts it out, a sudden glory of intimacy flinging yourself beyond yourself. So does your all-but-helpless flow of feelings toward another being—their suffering, the wondrous fact of them. It enjoys itself in your muscles as they stretch. It tastes every breath, even when you don't. It knows how much each thing completely matters. An imperturbable rightness is innate to what you touch when you touch emptiness.

Respond according to the emerging needs of the moment, complete with the moment. Such a willing disposition toward reality refuses all fixed agendas. When old (and I mean very old, somewhere between eighty and 120 years of age), Zhaozhou was asked, "What is your intention?" he assured the questioner (and us), "It has no method." First, I want you to practice this no-method. Second, I want you to practice it.

Try to find the method of the breaking waves conceding to the shore, the ripples in a river accepting a breeze. Without ducking the monk's deep desire to know Zhaozhou's mind, "It has no method" points beyond any possibility of well-planned routes to waking up. Every moment is that route. And Zhaozhou lays bare how to touch this and know it for yourself: Reality has no method. In fact, it has nothing at all.

Instead, you begin at every point, just like the Earth.

I swear the Earth shall surely be complete
To him or her who shall be complete,
And the Earth remains jagged and broken
Only to him or her who remains jagged and broken.[2]

To practice no-method is to follow the subtle contours of reality, which lie in no Procrustean bed. Procrustes was the mythological Greek innkeeper on a busy ancient Roman pilgrimage trail, overseeing an inn containing beds that no traveler could ever quite fit. So Procrustes simply cut the travelers down to fit the beds—not a very comfortable night's sleep!

Avoid all such beds! Not-knowing is exactly the skill of spotting and avoiding them. We will never sleep comfortably when trying to cut the whole, great, groaning Earth down to the size and shape of our frisky minds, which grab at panicked suppositions and fevered conspiracies.

"Do not find fault with the present moment" is Keizan's equally terse account of the logic of no-method. The walls come down, and we find we've always been at home right where we are. Keizan describes this mind of intimate accord as "empty and intelligent, alert and undazzled." There's the gift of not-knowing, lit by the alert and clear-eyed intelligence of emptiness, not easily dazzled by fear or dazzling itself with enlightenment.

Tuning into the constant flow, what is there to fault? Not even this foggy-minded self. Not-knowing relinquishes all that makes life too small, makes even death too small, and leaves Earth endangered. It is no-method to catch up with reality. Don't let Procrustes cut off your hands and feet.

Instead, cut off Procrustes: "Whatever confronts you, don't believe it!" That's the ninth-century master Yixuan Linji's version of Keizan's "no fault" and Zhaozhou's "welcome," recast as forensic not-knowing. This self is never more solid than when feeling confronted by crisis. Try setting aside what you immediately know to be confronting you, and then notice how it turns out to be the frame by which you've framed yourself.

With that gone, explore what remains as the open field of possibilities and actions that lie before you. It can be unexpectedly wide, surprising, and fertile.

Any crisis burns through all habitual assumptions like sun through fog. In the crises of mind that koans provoke, the first to go is the assumption of a weighty, bounded, separate self. When we realize this miraculous body-mind cannot possibly be carved *out of* the whole Earth and all other beings, then as long as there are mountains and rivers, oceans and beings, the Earth has a fighting chance to save us. We'll be present, seeing one another and hearing the call of the Earth more clearly.

To save the Earth, just risk at last belonging to it, being complete with it.

CODA: PRAISE IT

When Captain Ahab and the crew of the whaleship *Pequod* sighted the great white whale Moby-Dick for the first time, the men came to him terrified. "We asked the captain what course of action he proposed to take toward a beast so large, terrifying, and unpredictable. He hesitated to answer, and then said judiciously, "I think I shall praise it."[3]

What a fine statement of arrival at the vulnerable heart of resilience as it tilts toward wonder, acceptance, and fitness for purpose. This is fear becoming praise in a wonderfully lunatic move of the heart that puts aside knowing and dwells more closely to an open kind of prayer.

On a planet like this we're born precariously mortal. And let's widen the frame and see ourselves born into a universe—the very provenance of life and consciousness—that is itself a revelation of infinite precariousness. Each of us is already most unlikely. Each one is here only because one in many millions of spermatozoa chanced its way into an ovum deep in the body of a warm human being, one healthy and willing to carry gestation to term.

That warm human body of your mother existed only by way of infinite lucky chances of ancestral survival, an infinite regression going back to before the emergence of human beings. And you can walk on, praising, further back, beyond even that, to ancestors beyond ancestors, all the way to the rocks and waters of Earth, which already hold in their elements the mysterious potential that is you.

And Earth herself is so amazingly unlikely, a rare to impossibly sweet spot in the universe for life to become animate matter and bodies to animate complex consciousness. All this is from the raw elements born from cataclysmic stellar death, in the form of a smallish planet spun off from a medium-sized star, in a backwater of a vast (yet comparatively medium-size) galaxy.

Earth is one of the few solid rather than gaseous planets in our solar system, sufficiently cooled to form a thin crust, but sufficiently weighty, with its core of iron in both cooled and molten form, to keep gravitational hold on a thin atmosphere. At the same time, she possesses just enough of a cooled crust to slow interior cooling to an extremely slow pace. The molten iron, thus contained, swirling and rising to be cooled again, creates the magnetic field that shields Earth's life from harmful solar particles and activates electromagnetic navigation pathways in the brains of many creatures.

All of this unlikelihood is spinning with a very slight but seasonally productive wobble through the immensity of space. We are a whim of a capriciously changing but naturally resilient planet that gives birth to life that loves to live as long as she lives.

We animals of Earth live in precariousness on a planet due to be swallowed in a few billion years by our slowly dying sun. We human beings walk upright with knee joints not even remotely designed for bipedal locomotion, obliged to live aware that as surely as you are here, one day this unrepeatable "you" will be dust or less.

The lunacy and wonder of it! To be born in a mortal body of mortal parents, daring to love other mortal people on a wondrous planet, in a mysterious universe, with conscious awareness of all of this—can we value and accord with this, the very element in which life swims? Because that is to praise it and live within this praise.

The cluster of emergencies within the climate tragedy gather as the physical and spiritual crisis of our times. How dead we've held the living Earth to be. Our world may be on the brink of an extinction as throughgoing as the dinosaurs or the ancient Persian empire. It's a time when all shock value has been drained from the word *unprecedented*.

Yet the precariousness of crisis is one teaching upside down. Try "welcome," it whispers. Choose what is. Celebrate how it calls on you to pay closer attention. To choose uncertainty will open your heart to loss, touch your own mortality, and embrace the sorrow of lost expectations. Then can even grief become the path on which we're led to heal the Earth?

Unexpectedly, this empty, openhanded state turns out to be exceptionally well-provisioned for the long human work of deep, sustaining adaptation, for it is self-relinquishment that welcomes us into readiness.

wildflowers bloom in what's left of hope

火

3

A FIRE RUNS
THROUGH ALL THINGS

I'm going to try speaking some reckless words,
and I want you to try to listen recklessly.

—ZHUANGZI

There's a potent story in Rumi's epic poem *The Masnavi* in which a farmer goes out at night without a lantern to check on the ox in the barn. The dear, reliable ox he knows so well stands patient and unquestioning in the dark. He pats its huge shoulder and leans confidently against its warmth, completely unaware that a lion, having eaten his ox and taken its place, is now standing silently where the ox was tethered.

The farmer would die on the spot if he knew he was so blithely patting down this inconceivable reality.

Awakening is a kind of death, the fortunate death of all dividedness.

A SOLITARY BRIGHTNESS

Linji said, "There is a solitary brightness without fixed shape or form. It knows how to listen. It knows how to understand. It knows how to convey the teaching. That solitary brightness is you." The world can fall away to show its true, unvarnished face at any time. When I was seven years old I was snatched from what most call "reality" and seized by a vision that opened of its own accord in the course of the most ordinary of moments.

I was on my way to the girls' toilet in the playground of my small school in Cairns, barefoot as always, picking my way down the little informal "pathway of desire," as planners call such shortcuts as this, worn through the grass at the back of the toilet block. I remember the prickly sensitive plants drooping their fronds where I brushed them, the chanting of the nine-times multiplication table floating from some classroom. I may have been humming a little as you do in that swim of dreamy observation when I was stopped in my tracks by an experience that replaced everything around me.

Abruptly, suspended in vast, dark space, I found myself blazing, a body of radiance, pouring out in fathomless darkness. Later I'd compare it to being "like a star" because what else comes close? But this vast state sustained no name, object, subject, gap, or difference anywhere in the universe. And this also was me. Like nothing else at all.

Amazement arrived in waves: First, electrified, glad shock—so this is what we are! Then, the simple great joy of recognition—of course we are this! A tipping point in consciousness that tipped me out, vast and free!

Many years later, the words of Hongzhi found and named me in that moment: "The body is not a collection of atoms but a stately wondrous being. The mind is not emotional and intellectual entanglements, but an unknowable, solitary awareness."

Slowly, the presence of other such bodies of fire swam into sight in the dark, warm, utterly receptive empty space. It was plain to my seven-year-old mind, which you'd call ecstatic except that it was also calmly plain that all beings were this, too, all things exactly this. It just was. Is. Adding anything to it is absurd. Impossible to say how long I stood there suspended, spellbound, streaming with it. There was no time, no words. A vision requires someone to be gazing at something, but this no-me was not looking at, but *from* and *as* the light pouring out, blazing and inexhaustible. I knew myself and all that is to be utterly safe, whatever may happen—a perfect fit with reality, an extraordinary confiding, a reassurance so utter that it still brings tears to my eyes.

Young children are immensely practical, so in good time I just came back to myself, enough to attend to the call of nature and then go back to my classroom—just a small girl passing through an ordinary school day, which of course I was. I rode my small bike home that afternoon, heart still too big to fit in my chest, everything amazed yet manageable and in place.

The joy of it, so huge! How much there was no me! How much no-me there was!

I felt a child's duty to tell my parents about it despite sensing that it could not fit words. I found my mother in the kitchen, chopping carrots for dinner. I tried something tentative like, "Mum, isn't it amazing what we are!" She considered this lovingly, continuing to chop, chop, chop, and I could feel the great business already failing to make its way across to her as she finally said something like, "Yes darling, it's very good we're all so lucky we have one another, we all love one another, and . . ."

Which was true and very good indeed, but could not touch it, not at all. Something advised me to tuck undivided reality safely away where nothing could harm it except trying to talk about it. That silence would look after it best. And so instead of trying any further, I ran out lightly to swing on the trapeze and roman rings in our backyard with my sister, in the lovely last of the light.

That fundamental childhood moment went on in time to draw me to the rigor of Zen practice. Other experiences confirmed it, none exactly the same as any other. The fire that runs through all things blazes up just as and where it will; it has no method, but no objection to a degree of rigor either. It's what a seven-year-old drops into with almost matter-of-fact ease, while a more burdened adult has a lot of knowing to get past before they can recover a child's ability to rely on just what is happening, conceding this self to each thing just as it is, whether sunlight, heat, nine times nine is eighty-one, bird squawk, light fingers of wind parting the hair, smell of mud with faint whiff of urine, or the rapture of knowing yourself complete on this radiant and infinitely detailed Earth.

INTIMATE AND AWAKE

"I came to see that mind is no other than the mountains, the rivers, the great wide Earth, the sun, the moon, and the stars," said Dogen after his great experience of body and mind dropping away. Since the fire that created the universe runs also through us, how does that fact influence the great crisis that now lies before we human beings? Can we bring this mind to meet a world on fire?

Yes, for our anguish for the Earth and our power to take part in her healing arise from the same source: this singular heart-mind, intimate and awake.

Crises, like the tiny art forms of not-knowing that are koans, huge inside, do not explain or lend themselves to the known, which they disrupt. Rumi's farmer went out with no lamp in hand. Not supposing anything, trusting the dark, he chanced to touch the inconceivable, a life-resolving glimpse of the nature of reality that holds as exactly empty and equal the ox, the barn, the dirt on the floor, the broom in the corner, the cobwebs in the roof, and the owl in the rafters crunching the bones of a mouse. And a chance for astonishing awakening. All run as fire through you and all things.

"What is this?" the lion asked the farmer's fingers as he rubbed down what he supposed to be his ox.

Crises and koans alike ask, "What is this?" Each one is a chance to tenderly and somewhat anxiously pat down the shoulder of what you take to be the known and truly wonder "What is this?" "This" is the inconceivable reality, ordinary and absolute, undivided; it is equally ordinary ox and inconceivable lion, like you and me; it is the Milky Way and the swirl of rain and leaves in a gutter.

The mind that comes armed with knowing can only reconfirm *ox* as it leans obliviously into *lion*. Koans concede nothing to the linear mind and leave no choice but to let go of fear in the greater intimacy of not-knowing. Their small, homeopathic doses in the face of mental paralysis shift us beyond fear to make the transformational business of Rumi's lion their own. Their formidable resistance to what we think we know is what makes space in us to allow us to touch what lies beyond all supposition. Thus can we free-fall through fear of tragic failure, ruin, death, and extinction into the fullness of reality. And we get to work from there.

Everything happening is "one long rehearsal for your freedom," as Australian poet Les Murray (1938–2019) recognized even in the sound of an owl in the rafters crunching mouse bones. Why keep it waiting?

NOT WAITING

Mortality walks and breathes with us all our lives, though we mostly keep our backs turned pointedly away from its steady companionship.

A Zen student, bothered by growing slowly more aware that her death was no longer over the hills and far away, finally agreed to summon the courage to speak directly to the oppressive presence death was becoming for her. She chose a moment when she was driving through the foothills of Mount Wellington (increasingly called by its Palawa name, *kunanyi*), the magnificent guardian mountain that rises protectively behind Hobart. Gathering all her daring, she mentally invited her death to sit right there in the passenger seat beside her as she drove. And when the time and courage finally came, she said out loud, "Hello my death."

"And how did death reply?" I asked.

"Death said, 'Hello my life!'" she said, and broke into gales of laughter. Just two old friends it turned out, heading off somewhere together.

Offering the intimate, first-person possessive *my* to *death* immediately bestowed its blessing back on her life. That conversation sang the matter up in the dual first-person dialogical style that cheeky Aboriginal philosopher Tyson Yunkaporta dubs "us-two." Us-two—two that are very much not two—can shake awareness free from the knowing-in-advance that presumes to replace the discoveries of this life. She drove on in that very daring form of us-two, the vividness of her life lit up in the mirror of her inconceivable death. Not presuming her way into the darkness of its strange provenance, she was simply freed into its presence. Into presence, itself.

The brightness of all that is rests on the inconceivable darkness of the dark. The eighth-century English monk Saint Bede depicted this life as a swift bird who accidentally flies in from the darkness through one fortuitously open window in a great hall. Finding the hall laid out with an astonishing banquet, the tiny bird sweeps amazed through the brilliantly lit space, drinking in the spectacle of bejeweled guests, abundant food, and wondrous music, before—almost accidentally and too soon—coming to one far window, also fortuitously left open, and before it is possible to have any second thoughts, slips back into the vast, boundless darkness. For Saint Bede, our astonishing interval of life is but one brilliant flash of mystery briefly provisioned by the infinite resources of a greater mystery deeply at rest in an infinite darkness. The bird's trajectory and our life's trajectory swoops through the brilliant world of form on fire with emptiness.

Another woman I know dreamt of being caught in a storm and seeking shelter with her partner and stepchild in what looked something like a storm drain on a hillside, though up close it proved to be a natural formation lined with soft green moss that glowed. Gradually it grew on her that the light was subtly different at either end of this green "birth canal" shelter—opaque at one end, translucent at the other. Lightning flashed, and suddenly she wondered with panic whether she would know which end to go out of when the storm finally subsided. She somehow knew that one end was birth, the other end death, but also that she had no idea which was which.

The terror! What if she chose wrong?

"At that moment," she wrote, "an understanding—not exactly a voice, but a knowing—enters the stone womb with the words, *It doesn't matter. Birth and death are the same.* I feel tremendous relief. I know it to be the truth. And that is when I wake up, in the dream, and in my dreamer's bed."

Waking up is the profound reconciliation of birth and death, a strangely simple, oddly familiar reconciliation, one that radically enlivens this life. Emptiness resolves bright and dark, life and death, as no longer two and even less than one.

BRIGHTNESS AND DARKNESS

Here is Yunmen, in Case 86 of *The Blue Cliff Record*, offering his own instruction for recognizing the fullness of that lion standing silent in that dark barn: "Everyone has their own light. If you want to see it, you can't. The darkness is dark, dark. Now, what is your light?"

There laid out is the entire process of walking with intent into the empty dark. It's a process that takes courage to calmly doubt all that we think we know and lay aside all that forces a gap, until no barrier remains to the direct touch of reality. The fourteenth-century theologian and mystic Meister Eckhart confirmed this profound "no gap" when he said, "The eye through which I see God is the eye through which God sees me." If you want to see it, you can't.

But the courage needed derives from the profound reassurance that "everyone has their own light," our own personal access to it in our own distinct shape.

Such reassurance is also a challenge, for Yunmen just said you already have what it is that you seek in the darkening darkness. So how will you find what you seek? He offers nowhere to move, either forward or backward. Can you make yourself available to what lies beyond the reach of wanting anything at all?

Yunmen's resonant description of the necessity to give away all your possessions and stand empty of all ideas comes next: "Everything is dark, dark."

"Dark" in this case is another way of saying "empty." Everything empty, empty. Can you sense the rich state of not supposing and no expectations here, an exhilarating state of trepidation and trust?

Rumi's lion roars in Yunmen's next words: "Now, what is your light?" *Now*—not just any time . . . what do you think your light might be? Now! Your original nature, what is it?

At this point, move an inch and you'll break in two. It seems the assembly to which Yunmen was speaking was holding its collective breath, because he goes on to answer his own question: "The storeroom. The gate," he says. The ox in the barn, for that matter, and the owl chewing mouse bones; the box of discarded cabbage leaves in the waxed cardboard box, waiting to go to the chickens; the afternoon breeze idly stirring the bushes; the dog sleeping a few feet away, perky shadow of the wren by the water bowl; the mourning that Earth's fate rests in shaky, obdurate human hands, together with squawks from the gang of parrots gorging on the ripe mandarin tree. *Your light.*

The unadorned thusness of just what Is, Its ringing detail beyond better or worse, beyond praise, is the moment the thinking mind relaxes. The burning bush that Moses saw—we now see that every bright, distinct thing burns with this all-consuming fire.

HAVING NOTHING

Even after making it as daylight plain as this, Yunmen growls out a few more words to wipe away all remaining trace of preferencing, holiness-making, or self-adornment: "It would be better to have nothing than something good."

That "nothing" restores the morning breeze. It moves freely among all things, preferencing all, finding each thing best. The fire of emptiness is beyond good and not good; all things are equal in its fire, and it cannot be a thing to possess when it leaves nothing out.

Yunmen is no friend to the "having" urge in us. Friend only to the boundless no-thing that you and all beings share, he scotches every impulse and dream of having or not having what is already completely you. This great matter is in reach of no preferences and lies before time, always coming down exactly to now. A most stringent understanding, it can't be forced any more than the bare, dark branches of the apricot tree in winter can be forced into blossoming. But Yunmen's "dark, dark" insistently points the way to realize our one vast, shared, solitary light.

"Truly, is anything missing now?" asks seventeenth-century Zen master Hakuin Ekaku, in his "Song of Zazen." In that dark, dark that manifests itself bright, bright in every form, the discovery that truly nothing is missing is the shock that resounds throughout the universe. When preferences go dark and lie quiet, everything is moving in reach. The choice of not-knowing and no-preferences has a playful aspect with immeasurable creative pay-off. "Play it sideways, use it upside down"—this is the spirit of koans.

Whatever we seek to have, possess, or keep slips right through our fingers like water. "Having nothing" is at last arriving complete in the midst of all that we've ever had in this passing-through world. Zazen aligns you with this generous, flowing stream of "having nothing." And fearlessness and equanimity in meeting and acting on our circumstance all our days have their source in this realization.

A THEOREM OF EMPTINESS

In the third century, the Indian philosopher Nagarjuna dissolved the delusion of a separate self by comprehensively dissolving into each other the "two truths," or two accounts of reality that side by side appear irreconcilable, yet verify each other completely. He established that the truth of ordinary perceived reality is not other than ultimate reality, and that the truth of ultimate reality is not other than ordinary perceived reality. Or later, as the Heart Sutra put it, form is exactly emptiness, emptiness is exactly form.

Perceived reality is the first truth—the shifting, loosely agreed-on consensus about "the way things are" that serves to make daily life sufficiently viable and is ultimately molded for us by the functions and the givens of a particular language. It simultaneously creates and confirms what is customarily held to be real.

Ultimate reality, the second truth, is unhindered by any of the characteristics we attribute to things and beings in this world. None of the dualistic thinking imposed on our world can touch, affect, or alter the inherently empty, seamless, unfixed nature that all things enjoy "from their own side," as Nagarjuna put it. His Madhyamaka, the "Middle Way" school of Mahayana Buddhism, takes the two truths into an exhaustive elaboration of fundamental emptiness, bringing the concept of no-thing to an analysis of the true nature of reality. Perhaps the school's most famous theorem of emptiness is expressed as a tetralemma—a fourfold proposition that, in this case, unfolds as a sequence of negations. The fourfold negation of Nagarjuna's tetralemma sets out the nature of fundamentally empty reality that burns up duality and heals all opposites back into each other, complete.

The four negations counterpose each other like this:

1. This is that, that is this, and so "Form is emptiness, emptiness is form." In other words, reality is not-two.
2. This is not that, that is not this, thus, "Form is not emptiness, emptiness is not form." In other words, reality is not-one.
3. (There is) no this, no that, thus, "(There is) no form, no emptiness." In other words, reality is less than one.
4. This is this, that is that, "Form is form, emptiness is emptiness." In other words, reality is numberless.

Rather than logically and sequentially contradicting one another, all four truths resolve to the singular truth of emptiness, in which no thing is fixed or enduring, all things are insubstantial and in flux, and thoughts, feelings, formulations, and propositions of self also share the nature of emptiness. The tetralemma formalizes the field of not-knowing that is our ground of personal experience of undivided reality, which is exactly what is here and now. I am born and will die; I am unborn and do not die. Emptiness can find no contradiction here.

The experience of emptiness leaves this intellectual-sounding set of propositions directly felt, bone-deep, and luminous. Practice means always coming down to this most basic fact in your own breathing body, not laboring through any kind of mental exercise.

These four faces of original, inexhaustible emptiness in which all forms rise and fall away can become abruptly plain in the simplest and most immediate of things, such as a sneeze heard in the dark, the impression of a tire track in soft earth, or the warmth of a kangaroo's body experienced in a dream. Any one of the "myriad things," as Dogen calls it, suddenly and mysteriously able to slip past a "separate" self, can confirm your true nature, which is a reunion marked by tearful joy and laughter. Suddenly, each thing, even including the self, appears shockingly complete and entire with the whole that we call "this" or "it," and even more shocking is that it always has been so. Elaboration beyond this point begins to push it away.

Our self-nature is boundlessly free; it defeats, empties, and laughs at every conceptual attempt to take hold of its undividedness. Ultimate reality heals the separations dreamed up by language, dissolves the illusion of things as having a fixed, unchanging nature. It confirms the boundless, interwoven quality of all things, illuminating how they stand in their own place so briefly, in one shared blaze of impermanence. The Bantu word *ubuntu* succinctly expresses the true condition of being human: "I am because we are."

That "we" is very big. Even earwigs and COVID-19 belong and are complete with it.

AN APPROPRIATE RESPONSE

Koans use words to wake us up to the fact that reality is unconfined by words; it is no intellectual matter to be "solved" with the mind. A koan is taken up, committed to heart, then lived with intently as it does what it does to rearrange you. In the process, not-knowing restores mind back to its original completeness, together with each particle of matter and each moment. Each time, in a shock that lights up understanding, we find emptiness engraved on our own bones and inscribed on the skin of all things. Our original blessing is requited in every breath of ordinary life.

Can familiarity with such a falling away of any sense of separation help ignite a more fearless and ready presence to meet the crises of our times? Does learning how to drop that beleaguered, separate "someone" and return to all that is here result in seeing more clearly what to do next? How does boundlessly free self-nature respond to catastrophic ecological collapse as we scramble the mind of our climate? Freed from the joyless suffocation of being confined to our own skulls, we can recognize ourselves to be interestingly woven into what is wanted, needed, and forming.

As humanity struggles to perceive and acknowledge inclinations that run so counter to the terms of the Earth, the hardest thing to overcome is fear—fear of ourselves, of the other, of scarcity and discomfort, of loss and mortality, of the Earth herself. And fear of the shame that this arouses.

Unaddressed, such fear makes us dangerous. It leaves us blind to reality and unable or unwilling to risk fully loving and trusting its great and mysterious forces (as though they were separate and opposed to this self). The most important social and spiritual movements in human history, according to Thomas Berry (1914–2009) are those that truly shape and give meaning to life because they bind the human venture to what he has termed "the larger destinies of the universe." In other words—and luckily—in the unavoidably sharp moments of human history we have had no choice but to more fully realize this business of being human.

Berry, a Catholic priest, cultural historian, and scholar of world religions and Earth history, saw the overarching demand of this time as no less than the reinvention of the human at the level of our species, with critical reflection, admitting our place within the community of life-systems. I especially appreciate his humble, clear-eyed demand for "critical reflection." *Critical* means thought prepared to place itself thoroughly in crisis, which is exactly the skill entrained and exercised by Zen koans.

The world is in an unprecedented crisis. We have no choice but to align and move with this reality if we are to survive, while finding a depth of adaptation that forms a path beyond mere survival. It is unrushed reflection that ushers in the means of our responding—the skillful not-knowing that frees the self to reopen its long, deep conversation with the Earth.

In Case 14 of *The Blue Cliff Record*, a monk asks Yunmen, "What is the teaching that Shakyamuni Buddha preached throughout his life?"

Yunmen replies, "One appropriate response." This statement can also be translated as "One teaching upside down," which makes perfect, enlivening sense in light of the path thus far walked in this book, for mind turned upside down shakes emptiness out of all of our pockets.

Just one appropriate response, for it manifests in each particle of matter and in each moment. There's nothing that can fall outside or fail to offer it; even the monk's searching question brings it forward. But Hakuin cautions us, saying, "Inaccessible beyond compare, this saying is horrendously stern."[1]

Why? Because it takes all that we humanly are to continue to meet the always unfolding offer of this singular reality. The appropriate response is all on us and our ability to relinquish ourselves.

Welcome to the willing choice of self-endangerment.

NOTHING AT ALL

Luna Park Sydney is a much-loved 1920s-era fun park set on the harbor, just to one side of the great arc of Sydney Harbour Bridge, which grins quizzically across the water at the great white cultural icon that is the Sydney Opera House. In earlier days it had a many-towered Coney Island–style fun castle filled with cheap thrills and certifiable wonders, such as the wooden slippery slides three stories high, down which you flew on burlap sacks at dazzling speeds. But the magnetic attraction at its heart was a musty, one-way maze of pitch-dark passageways. In that oddly too-warm, intestinal darkness, you inched along, blindly testing the walls for twists and sudden turns, scared, thrilled, always moving forward, when suddenly your foot inching forward encountered . . . *nothing*.

Nothing! No floor! Everything dark, dark . . .

Blindly probing that nothing, you would eventually discover some way down an unreadable kind of queasily squishy surface, a ground of pure uncertainty in pitch-black darkness. To proceed there was no choice but to gingerly lower yourself down and trust your weight to it until you bumped once more into the big step back up and onto solid floor. It is impossible to forget the electrifying thrill of suddenly confirming that there is nothing to rely on and, ultra-aware as you blindly hazard the next step, and the next, that not-knowing is a most intimate state of being.

The realm of childhood play is where we initially learn the intense reward of stepping through the fear of not-knowing and turning it around to just *use* it, instead. All play lives on that creative edge. So often people report that the depths of zazen in long silent retreats reawaken a child's simple, visceral joy in unmediated communing with just what is, with no gap. How exhilarating it is to recover the sheer relish of approaching that place of no separation, like a very young child running down the beach toward waves, singing out, "I am the beach! I am the waves! I am the seagulls!"

Wonder unleashed, entirely befitting a miracle such as Earth— we play with it freely as children but generally have to work against the grain of all our adult knowing to recover that skill of openness. Zazen is one method for its recovery and enjoyment. That's where you willingly place yourself at the best kind of risk, to turn trepidation around into a steady form of attention that aims only to arrive in the place where you are, at last.

WHO DARES?

Zen is deeply playful in its serious intent. No-mind has no ground to stand on, nowhere to fall. The intuitive moves of play open exactly here.

Play is our way of being safely reckless with fixed, dead-serious views, especially the very self-important ones. Many Zen expressions of awakened joy gleam with the light of playfulness:

- "Walking alone in the red sky"
- "Riding the winged horse backward"
- "Fish all the oceans with a straight hook."
- "Who dares to tug the whiskers of the tiger?"
- "Then bring me the rhinoceros!"

Every koan dares to play with perceived reality and be at play in ultimate reality. Naturally, none take the road of explanation, which would steal the chance for the singular joy that can only be discovered on the crooked and intuitive path of not-knowing. English poet and artist William Blake (1757–1827) saw it clearly in *The Marriage of Heaven and Hell*: "Improvement makes straight roads, but the crooked paths without Improvement are paths of Genius."

Original nature cannot be improved. This truth proves wonderfully frustrating to the straightener and the planner. Koans draw us onto the crooked path, each step in the dark lit up by the always unexpected intelligence of emptiness.

TIPPING POINTS

We are playing such intensely reckless games with climate tipping points: melting sea ice absorbs more sunlight, leading to more melting sea ice; shrinking forests produce less rain, which further shrinks the forests; thawing permafrost releases methane, which further thaws the permafrost. The corrective, restorative tipping point in consciousness that koans recklessly trigger is an offer worthy of close attention and one that we cannot afford to refuse. For the valuable jolt of fundamental sanity that koans deliver to the heart and mind can help land us back in an undivided state that is more complete with the Earth.

Interestingly, the archaic word *reck* means "care," as in heeding and taking care of what is most important. Thus to be reckless is to be rash, impetuous, heedless of the consequences of your actions. Zhuangzi's "I'm going to try speaking some reckless words, and I want you to try to listen recklessly" playfully pushes reckless over, exposing its underbelly of "reck" as profound care. To listen recklessly is therefore to abandon the imposture of already starting forward with knowing and to lean back into the "reck" of a radically open mind.

Koans are not interested in smoothing out gnarly reality; they freely enter the mishmash of this world, setting fire to all presumptive certainties. The inconceivable stands up in the ordinary, mixed, earthy mystery of life itself and nowhere else. A koan considers you to be naturally designed to be hit between the eyes by ultimate reality, heart receptively bare, hands empty and ready. Each one brings forward the Dharma in a singular fragment of complete reality, absent all handholds.

"Dear incomprehension, it's thanks to you I'll be myself in the end."[2] Samuel Beckett's words admit, albeit with a considered measure of ironic twentieth-century despair, that the mysterious depth of this self can never be confirmed with what we believe we already comprehend. Yet his words mirror Mazu's sturdy encouragement from the traumatic depths of eighth-century China: "The mind that doesn't understand—that's exactly it!" To really understand life and death, just silently observe the moment before thoughts are born. That moment is wide-open.

Every koan points to the heart of the one who wonders, "What is this self?" A desire to realize the edgeless self is reckless in the best way, and zazen is where you can dare wonder, supposing nothing. Emptiness confirms even the unsettled state of your own heart as complete beyond praise or blame. And in your heart of hearts, there is no need to name what appears, or agree or disagree with it. Nothing sticks to "who" when it is not locked into "I."

When a woman asked Zhaozhou, "What is this?" he placed the question back into all our hands by replying, "The heart of the one who asks." He is not deflecting a heartfelt question about the nature of the boundless reality brimming in every detail of *this*. Even the unsettled state of your own uncertain heart is a gateway. "Enter here," he suggests.

MU: REALIZING THE INCONCEIVABLE

Perhaps the most reckless word ever offered in the annals of Zen is Zhaozhou's *Mu*. Welcome to the thinking mind turned upside down.

To take up Mu (*Wu* in Chinese) as a koan is to take one syllable to which nothing can be attached and then let it undo every means by which you've made yourself up. To do this wholeheartedly leaves you ablaze in the emptiness that streams like dark matter through all that is.

The inside story of emptiness? Nothing exists except in relation to everything else. The experience called "waking up" or "realization" is the burning up of all separation in the clear nature of all that is. Awakening is the most extravagant gesture this extravagant universe can make toward a willing human being who is longing to arrive here, home, complete on the Earth.

Mu is one small word that marks the spot where "I" disappears only to turn up in all that is. It can't be translated anymore than you can be, but hints of it lie in words like *no, not, undone, unmade, un-self, no-thingness, emptiness, absence.* Absent, at last, this all-enveloping self, and so, at last, *here.*

Often called "the first gate of the practice," Mu, just one syllable short of complete silence, is a straightforward no-gate to the inconceivable. And to our resounding shock, the inconceivable turns out to know you better than you know yourself. This magisterial koan drops into our laps from an inconsequential-looking exchange, once more between a monk and Zhaozhou, with possibly a dog somewhere nearby to help.

The monk asks, "Does a dog have buddha nature or not?"

Zhaozhou responds in one word: "Mu," throwing us a lifetime bone to chew all the way through. Just one word, so recklessly close to no words at all: "Mu."

With that one word he wiped away Zhaozhou, having, not having, monk, dog, you, me, and even Mu itself.

A koan that asks about a dog is of course a koan about the one who asks. How do I get free? That monk is asking or pleading or defensively checking. Dogs had a dubious status in old China, and this seems to be a monk anxious about his enlightenment status. Buddha nature is the original, nonnegotiable reality of this self and all that is. If a mangy dog has it, then do I? Or not?

But Mu does not know. It turns back and undoes every

knowing that would divide what is undivided. Mu gradually mutes the mind's tendency toward words. As Xuedou (980–1052) says in *The Blue Cliff Record*, "When mouth tries to speak about it, words fail. When mind wants to relate to it, thoughts fail." Nothing sticks to Mu. It's a no-word that opens to a strangely homely, wordless darkness. Words die there, thoughts fall apart, and something that's been ever-present but obscured can at last draw breath.

We approach the sacred mystery of reality through a door of silence and muteness, and this door swings open in its own good time and lets us step free. Then you will know how to stroke a no-dog: no-me, no-dog, just stroking, easing, softly groaning, stretching, warm, no-other.

If you have ever heard the Heart Sutra chanted in Sino-Japanese, you'll have heard how *mu mu mu mu* reverberates like a heartbeat: *no eye no ear no nose no tongue no body no mind*. This is where we find ourselves, amazed and beyond glad. *No* is a word you can fall right through, fully equipped for life yet minus thought, hands, eyes, feet, and so on.

How totally and cheerfully the word *no* rebuffs every attempted add-on. Writer and translator David Hinton favors *absence* as a telling alternative to rendering Mu/Wu as "empty" or as "no-thingness."[3] But *absence* comes close to implying something that was or should be here and is found to be missing, whereas *empty* has nothing missing or able to be added from the beginning. *Presence* carries the beautiful charge of realized mind; it is form charged with emptiness, which requires *absence* to be equally charged with form, so that emptiness and form reveal each other. But *absence* as a word does not quite possess that charge, while *no* says quite forcefully, "Don't. Just don't!" To all the default moves of mind that Mu cuts off, *absence* lingers a little too long, being a bit too philosophical (and possibly pleased with itself).

There is no number, no end, no barrier, no beyond to this empty fullness of where and what we are and have always been: each thing is marvelously singular (no number); this seeing through the barrier of the self is ceaseless (no end); this mysterious self is actually transparent to all that is (no barrier); and being here, awake in this mortal body, is complete (no beyond).

UNDONE

Whether or not you take Mu as your koan, the practice of Zen is resolutely the practice of not-knowing that has nothing to fix, improve, blame, push away, or fear. This leaves you with no one to do the fearing. This bare self stands mysterious, unmediated by words or mental constructs, immediate, beyond all thoughts, and *here*. Presence—as inarguable as flame.

The closest word for this undone state of presence is *intimacy*. You become nothing but direct touch—skin to skin—when no longer subtly forcing any self-preserving gap. And the touch is resoundingly mutual: as you accept, so you let yourself in to the acceptance that comes to meet you. And as you welcome, so you know yourself welcome in the unfolding fullness of what is no-me.

If you keep the loving, loyal compact with every moment that is practice or "attention," attending it, tending the mind that does not know, then when it's ready you will find Mu waiting for you. Pretty pleased to see you, in fact.

Mu is a greatly compacted expression of the whole universe that is our own self-nature. But Mu will never do your bidding. It's a valuable torment, this one, the desirable, unscratchable itch. What is Mu? What is this? Who is this? Every mental move you make toward it is a marvelous error. Until you know only that you can't say. But rest assured, at some point this state of being implacably blocked shifts and is suddenly interesting, freeing, even oddly comfortable. You have ceased dreaming of talking up reality or making reality conform to your own small wishes, plans, or bargains. Now you can go about taking Mu like a joyful torch to everything you experience.

You let the no-dog in to gulp down its no-breakfast. You look into the mysterious no-faces of other people. Your own face in the mirror, seen for the first time: a no-you. What if nothing is what you think or can think? Strangely vivid and alive, not alarming. Barriers are falling in the dark. Philosophers flee the scene, seeking refuge in the known.

Instructions like "Nothing but Mu" or "Only take hold of Mu" can appear to call for a busy, vigilant, self-suspicious self. But no. Luckily, no. "If you try to direct yourself, you deviate." Effortful intention subsides into a willingness to let Mu solely hold you, becoming the constant murmur of your own heart saying "no," "not," to every attempt to recruit Mu back to your own small story of the self.

NO-GATE

Gradually or suddenly, there's no significant "you" to speak of left in a seamless world. In J. D. Salinger's short story *Teddy*, a ten-year-old child watches his little sister gulp down a glass of milk and finds himself suddenly knowing he is watching her, as he puts it, pour God into God.[4] Call it Mu pouring Mu into Mu.

I once overheard a chatty woman in the seat behind me on a bus loudly endow everyone with a helpful prompt on the path of Mu. "I found myself coming over all unnecessary!" she informed her unseen companion. Mu catches you in that act over and over again and kindly suggests that *not* coming over all unnecessary might be, well, the one appropriate response.

"Not that way!" says Mu. Or just, "Not!" or "Don't," Mu explains, deepening attention just in time, over and again. You could almost call "Don't!" the complete advice sheet for working with Mu. Undo the self. Give it a rest, and see what is constantly filling your empty and astounded hands when you do.

Zhuangzi said, "You've heard of using wings to fly, but have you heard of using no-wings to fly? You've heard of using knowing to know, but have you heard of using not-knowing to know? Gaze into that cloistered calm, that chamber of emptiness where light is born." And where the emergent is always gestating.

Mu is the no-gate, wide as the universe, with no-barrier suspended in front of you on its no-hinges. It is transparent—often you can see the sun, the moon, and the stars visible through it, as well as the lines on your own face, the sorrow in the eyes of your neighbor, the devastation wrought in bushfire country, the collapsing hospitals of the pandemic surge, the broken buildings and crushed lives of war. Everything flows through this gate unimpeded.

The only obstacle is this self. The only recourse is seeing right through it. And then there is no barrier at all, though you will never cease catching yourself in the act of erecting one.

THE TIGER'S WHISKERS

As for instructions for Mu, here's the simple no-method: work, live, breathe with Mu as the gift of your own un-doing. Drop preferences. Drop expectations. Drop all escape attempts. Welcome not-knowing while cleaving to Mu with trust and persistence.

For encouragement you can perhaps add, "Do not regret your life!" or "What is this in the light of my death?" The whole enterprise is wonderfully reckless, worth betting your life on. Worth the (considerable) price of admission: just this self. Forgetting the self so thoroughly is daring to grab the tiger's whiskers. It's knowing that you touch the shoulder of the lion. It's celebrating your lunacy as one long, deep, unqualified prayer of "Help!" It's letting yourself become more like this, healing the gap between all the many beings. Then whatever you do helps.

But be fully warned: once you've been brushed by the tiger's whiskers, no comfortable assumptions will ever let you be quite as comfortable again. Examining your life in the constant face of increasing climate catastrophe becomes the prickling, awakening fire. Sweating the small stuff or drawing the protective covers over your head is unacceptable as soon as you catch yourself doing it.

What will you do *now*, now that you have been gathered in and standing apart is no longer comfortable or even an option? What is the work that our time asks of us?

CODA: YOUR ORIGINAL FACE
HAS NOWHERE TO HIDE

Who can look up at the starry fire of a night sky and miss the charged extravagance of this vast universe? Just as rocks, lichen, rivulets, sticks cracking underfoot, parrot squawks, shadows on the floor all reveal this mind, so do the stellar cataclysms that released the elements that brought all this to be, all of it—your original face together with civilizational suicide and the tragic possibilities of our times, which are burning through the haze of distractibility on a daily basis, scorching hearts and minds.

Earth is littered with the remnants of prehistoric, vanquished human worlds gone to dust, and the historic record carries the vivid story of self-destructive tendencies in human civilizations all the way up to now. That's it, too! Wumen's (1183–1260) verse to Case 23 of *The Gateless Barrier* declares:

It can't be described, it can't be pictured,
It can't be praised enough—stop groping for it.
The original face has nowhere to hide.
When the world is destroyed, it is not destroyed.

If you've glimpsed this face that has nowhere to hide, then a question like, "Can it really come to an end?" grows very wide. Does emptiness know "destroyed" and "not destroyed"? Regarding the night sky, have you anywhere to hide your original face, your entire body? There's an invitation to move with the wonder . . .

You are as numberless as the stars in the sky, as numberless as the creatures lost in the great funerary fires of a heating planet, as numberless as the faltering doubts and fears that flicker through you for the children and the unborn every day. And you, like a skink in the sun or a wombat chewing grass or a mosquito droning in the dawn, are no-number, a one-off, here in your own right and empty of any separation, any gap, from all that is. No number, numberless, complete.

In Case 29 of *The Blue Cliff Record*, a monk asks Zen master Dasui Fazhen (878–963), "When the universe is destroyed in the fire at the end of the universe, will this be destroyed or not?" Dasui says simply, "Destroyed." This "destroyed" is as uncompromising as Zhaozhou's "Mu," equally destroying both "destroyed" and "not destroyed."

And so a question about a universe-ending fire confirms the self-nature that does not know "perishable" or "imperishable." Dasui's "destroyed" is thorough and seamless. This profligate, fiery cosmos has no trace of "universe" or "self" anywhere in it. Realization heals the discriminating mind back to this and welcomes us home, undivided.

When the monk asks doubtfully, "It goes along with that?" Dasui confirms, "It goes along with that." Fire goes along completely with what it is burning. Emptiness goes along completely with universe, with water, with broken toenails, with the way the chirp of a bird darkens the eyes of a cat . . .

And mind goes along with universe. It goes along with the cosmic fire of the universe—its cataclysms, its vast creativity, its endurance, its shimmer, its poignant and ruthless beauty. The cosmic fire is the source of all that is, including this mind, just as it is the source of this ordinary, bumbling life. No talk anymore about enlightenment or delusion. Anything that would divide the undivided? Destroyed!

Your original face has nowhere to hide in this extravagantly combustible, impermanent, timeless reality. As Heraclitus said, "It ever was, and is, and shall be ever-living Fire, in measures being kindled and in measures going out."[5]

Emptiness is the original, unchanging, inconceivable nature of reality that burns in each particle of matter, each moment of this minutely interconnected flow of manifesting form we call Earth, cosmos, body, being. Emptiness is alight in every glowing detail of this world as well as the one called "you." We are flint as well as tinder for this fire. Are we capable of awakening into it? As we warm the air and seas and put a combustible world ever more at risk, can we dare consider that we are also, as Thomas Aquinas observed, *Capax universi*—"capable of the universe are your arms as they move with love."

We are not only the product of the deep creative energies of the universe; we cannot help but embody them, and we can learn to bring them forward creatively. We're here at the pleasure of primordial cataclysms of stars that are exploding at the end of their lives that were spent transforming hydrogen into helium. With the final great heating of a dying star, helium heats into the carbon that is matrix of all life, and then carbon into oxygen, iron, silicon . . . From such transformations comes the calcium in bone, the iron in blood, and the oxygen in the breath, heart, and lungs. Such a monumental cataclysm as the death of a star—or the waking up of a human being from the fear-based fortification of the separate self—is equal parts transformation, an opening to new domains of emergence, and the seeds of creative formation. This too is us.

"Awake" has no parts. Can we live this not-two, cultivating the field at every point for what is ripe for emergence? In a universe as impossibly vast and ruthless as this one, can you go along with it and let it flow in and out through your heart, hands, arms, and actions?

The fire at the end of the universe is distinctly echoed in the fire at the end of the small mind—one fire, running through all things. There is no gap between this humble mortal being and the creative, cataclysmic fire of the cosmos. It has nowhere to hide, and it is time to stop hiding from it.

charred into bark a gaze of fire

Part Two

MEDICINE AND SICKNESS HEAL INTO EACH OTHER

There's no cold spot in a boiling cauldron.

—XUEDOU

Why love what you will lose?
What else is there to love?

—LOUISE GLÜCK

火

4

LIVING IN A HOUSE ON FIRE

To be truly free, one must take on the basic conditions as they are,
painful, impermanent, open, imperfect. Be grateful for impermanence, and for the freedom it grants us.

—GARY SNYDER

Why, how, do we manage to turn our backs on the fullness of the
offer of this reality, this consciousness? The Buddha diagnosed
our self-created tendency toward feelings of lack and unease as a
sickness, one no human being has trouble recognizing. And he
prescribed its medicine: the four noble truths, which sketch out
the path of awakening.

Why this sickness? What is the full dimension of this recogniz-
able human unease, even disease, this "coming over all unnecessary" (as the woman on the bus informed her unseen companion)
that so easily sterilizes life of its joy and goes on to trample and
desecrate the living Earth?

And how are we to muster an appropriately fierce love for a
planet fast losing her ecological integrity in rising heat as she falls

into avoidable ruin? To the point where we are living in a house on fire, not just in the Buddha's sense of impermanence of body, world, and self, but tragically, in a way we are making absurdly literal. A sufficient evenness of mind and clarity of response in the midst of climate crisis has to be found here in the midst of the passionate nature of the human being.

These two streams of inquiry run through part 2, which searches out the subtle ways in which medicine and sickness not only heal each other back into one, but open a path in responding that is a path in fire.

———————

Forming strong attachment to what by nature cannot last and we cannot keep is Buddhism's early finding on the cause of avoidable suffering. The medicine offered is traditionally the Dharma of a cooled state of mind that clearly understands impermanence and has realized the pointlessness of desiring what cannot last.

But take care to be discerning here: while love is inclusive, desire is selective.

Early Buddhism longed to step free forever from the wheel of birth and death, but as we'll see, Mahayana Buddhism saw suffering very differently. Life cannot last, but renouncing all adherence to impermanent life comes dangerously close to detaching from all care for life. A practice of inclusion is a deeper, more challenging and transforming renunciation; it renounces not life, but the dream of a separate self, with its unending preferences that erode full presence to each other and the Earth.

Fire, as an evocation of impermanence and destructive impulses, runs through the Buddha's third sermon, known as the "Fire Sermon," delivered soon after his great awakening. Speaking to his followers at a place where fire was worshipped, he seized on that to depict the five senses as burning, igniting avoidable forms of suffering: "Burning with what? Burning with the fire of lust, with the fire of hatred, with the fire of delusion; with sorrow, lamentation, pain, displeasure, and despair, I say."

In the reasoning of the "Fire Sermon," to realise that clinging to what cannot last is the source of suffering is to become disenchanted with and coolly dispassionate toward all objects of desire born of the senses, thus extinguishing the fire of the passions and establishing the liberating peace of equanimity.

We are, however, in a very different geophysical moment to that of the time of the Buddha. Our time of planetary ecocrisis makes a profound call on the wise ability of our five senses to attune to the Earth and to each other. For it is our senses that attentively connect us to the infinite wonder and beauty of the living Earth, recharging our souls and healing and renewing our kinship with plants and creatures. Such renewal in turn inspires the kind of fierce and essential love that can shape right action on her behalf.

Composed centuries after the "Fire Sermon," the Lotus Sutra presents a parable of the world as a wealthy but decaying mansion filled with unresponsive children. The children are headdown over their toys and obsessions despite the warning of the wise old owner that they are trapped and living in a house on fire, a house with just one small exit that is also alight with impermanence. Escape is imperative, but no one moves an inch until they are told that outside the burning house is an unsurpassable toy—a huge and most wonderful oxcart adorned with unimaginable jewels (the "great vehicle" of the teaching that transcends suffering), at which point they all rush out and successfully free themselves.

But as chapter 5 explores, Zen, which formed centuries after the great Mahayana turn of the Dharma wheel, does not shrink from the passions or seek any cool remove from the world. Zen instead values most highly the lotus of awakening to no-self that blooms and is of service in the midst of the most challenging flames of this lifetime and this world.

WHY LOVE WHAT YOU WILL LOSE?

We are born and live and die by the grace of impermanence. By what other name can we call this unending change and transformation in which nothing lasts? Louise Glück takes impermanence head-on in her poem "From the Japanese," asking "Why love what you will lose?" The very next line becomes a koan that breaks the word *love* open into hot, bright coals: "What else is there to love?"[1]

Beautiful. Its truth runs both ways. All things pass through and cannot stay. There is nothing else to love but that which you will lose, including "you." And equally, what else could love possibly be but the beautiful, risky human willingness to commit to loving deeply what we also know will change and vanish?

Loss bestows the full measure and depth of love. When we cannot keep even ourselves from one moment to the next in this passing-through world, love takes no hostages against loss. Mourning is the final confirmation of the great depth of love. "We need, in love, to practice only this: letting each other go," wrote Rilke, "for holding on comes easily; we do not need to learn it."[2]

In this willingness to risk the potential agony of loss, there is already a loss of the self that is love itself, a love willing to be tested and confirmed in the fire of impermanence. This fire that runs through all things burns through life—in our suffering, in our losses, in our passions, and in our connectedness and mutuality, all of which is love itself. It offers as a strange blessing the fact that there is nothing to hang on to in impermanence, nothing to haggle with in emptiness. We can stop bargaining and start directly expressing the nature of the universe in acts of compassion and caring.

The way of radical acceptance cannot understand anything, including ourselves, to be inherently separate. Such a way evolves love in creative and affirming tension with vulnerability. Samsara and nirvana, sickness and medicine—these pairs are unopposed in emptiness but continually healing back into each other in human awakening: one blaze.

Zen finds the sacred order of things manifesting not in some safe elsewhere, but in impermanence itself. Suffering is, strangely, both sickness *and* medicine, impossible to tease apart in the end. Rather than medicine opposing sickness, emptiness sees in medicine and in sickness a mutual yielding and healing. That we suffer and share this great fact of impermanence together is profound medicine in itself, a medicine that releases compassion, love, connectedness, and forgiveness as the healing source.

The seamless fire of impermanence empties each entity of any kind of enduring substance, and this includes the self. Since all things, from the smallest particle of matter to the entire universe, share this temporary, passing-through existence, the small dream of separation can drop away into that fire of impermanence and discover there the extraordinary weave of interconnected life.

I once heard Aunty Beryl Carmichael, a Ngiyampaa elder in Darling River country in New South Wales, Australia, put it simply: "Reality is connectedness. If you're not in connectedness, you're not in reality." With a sustainable, living world at stake, this has become the severely urgent matter to realize and convey.

There's no set formula called "how to save the world." Connectedness can't be ordered up, laid out, or unraveled. Its fire runs through an infinite network of points of mutual contact and exchange that are beyond explanation and must simply be accepted with respect and gratitude. The direct experience of this mysterious, manifest connectedness is balm to the human heart and mind. Salvaging, restoring, and protecting life is strong medicine too, healing both the protectors and the protected.

Robert Hass, U.S. Poet Laureate from 1995 to 1997, once gave koanlike expression to our plight along the lines of: we are the only protectors, and we are what needs to be protected, and we are what it needs to be protected from. Yet the excruciating sharpness of the dilemma he sketched out has an exquisite roundness at its heart, for exactly equally, we cannot harm the Earth without harming ourselves; we cannot heal the Earth without healing ourselves; we cannot protect the Earth without protecting ourselves.

SICKNESS IS MEDICINE

A deep current of healing runs through the sickness that is our dream of separation and our corresponding capacity to inflict profound harm. To recognize that our infinitely interconnected world never stops flowing, is never finished, and so cannot be "fixed" begins to break the frame by which we have framed ourselves.

Hearing the Buddha's parable of the house on fire as described in the Lotus Sutra can jump-start the heart into action in these precarious times. In this case, the house is a metaphor not only for your body but also for all things of this world and all that you love and hold dear. Impermanence has no exceptions. In the words of Xuedou, "There's no cold spot in a boiling cauldron"—no place to retreat to, no way to hold on to anything at all. Impermanence is ablaze with emptiness and pervades the whole universe—unconditioned, unqualified, undivided, unsorted, and existing right here in this very moment of your being.

But don't miss the fact that a cauldron can also be a vessel of transformation.

It is profoundly mournful that the people, places, creatures, and things we love are destined to perish. Yet in perishing is found the spark of a complete yielding that ignites the truly imperishable glimpse of love. I am reminded of Dante's Pilgrim in the final line of each stage of the testing journey of *The Divine Comedy*, finding himself once more under the sheltering empty sky of "the love that moves the sun and the other stars." We come to where the sickness and its medicine heal each other, where impermanence and love are mutually resolved. For it is the fire of impermanence that reveals the healing and annealing fact of interwoven connectedness in the matter of always passing through, with everything moving *together*—very like an ecosystem!

Annealing implies that extreme heat must be exerted to alter the physical and sometimes chemical properties of a substance to make it more malleable and able to be drawn out without becoming brittle. The annealing quality of crisis appears when we face into the overwhelmingly painful fact and let it rearrange us and draw our hidden qualities out and into play. Crisis reveals the creative energies at play in times of dramatic change and softens the categorical beliefs that kept us painfully hardened and resistant, as time maintains its sacred right to meddle in all our affairs of love.

WORLD ON FIRE

In the season in hell that was the Australian six months of fire in 2019 and 2020, we were obliged to learn a newly coined word, *pyrocumulonimbus*, to name the towering thunderheads of superheated smoke that crowned the skies for months. These fire clouds were born of firestorms so intense they created their own weather system, producing freakish rainfall amid the dry lightning that continued to spark fresh outbreaks in advance of the massive fire front. This new word took its place in an uncanny new world where meaning has begun to slip many of its old constraints.

In the aftermath, walking with dread through the ravaged world left by the megafires, we tasted another neologism, *solastalgia*—grief for the loss of precious places, landscapes, creatures, and ecosystems. This word combines solace, desolation, and nostalgia to describe the indigestible sorrow for places desecrated by fires, floods, storms, drought, as well as the loss of habitat due to development.

"It's too much for the heart!" a fellow volunteer cried as we threaded vegetables onto wire wreaths and filled donated baby bathtubs with water to be set out for the wild creatures that survived out of the three billion that died in the firestorms. The climate crisis is at times simply too big to even dare see, overwhelmingly painful, and too threatening to all that we have previously known. In this way it is a *hyperobject*, philosopher Timothy Morton's term, coined for processes that unfold outside the scale to which human comprehension has evolved. New words for new situations our minds are loathe to scale, but now must...

A firewall of misinformation cynically designed to maintain damaging neglect and stifle the urgent need for action can obscure the enormity of the problem but cannot hold back the reality of an ancient methane world forced from its grave by warming temperatures. When that unstoppable megafire was moving toward my home in Australia, I quickly found out how fast it devoured expectations and burned through assumptions. A truthful, reality-based consensus became the sole trustworthy refuge for those experiencing the fire. We tuned to the unmistakeable new reality and we acted!

Yet, as we live into a time of accelerating climate collapse, as well as the changes wrought by pandemics and the economics of perpetual growth, the illusion of normalcy can muddy our response. The world is chaotically changing in plain sight, but doing so with just enough of a semblance of its former self to let us glance nervously off from it, as the days for mitigating its great harm grow very late.

HARD TO SEE IN PLAIN SIGHT

Meanwhile, the picture presented by climate modelling of global warming to the end of this century makes you feel accusing eyes from a ruined world looking back at us—at our devotional adherence to the path that we know is setting our home on fire and tearing down the web of life. The pressure of the looming crisis both highlights our mortality and sends a shudder of shame for the world we are leaving our descendants. Perhaps a shudder of remorse, too, for the indifference we've shown to the world passed to us by our ancestors.

The 1770 journal of Joseph Banks, who accompanied the explorer James Cook on the journey that partially mapped the east coast of Australia, offers a remarkable record of what it was like to sail right before open eyes regarding you from another time and world.

When the HMS *Endeavour* sailed into the part of what would later become Sydney that Cook dubbed "Botany Bay" (in honor of Banks, the ship's botanist), it was a wide, calm bay plush with mangroves that provided breeding grounds for plentiful fish. A group of Dharawal people were fishing with spears from the rocks. What slowly appeared and sailed past them, just yards away, was unthinkable: a small but elaborate wooden emissary from Enlightenment Europe, mounted with sails, manned with small cannon, navigated with instruments that read (and mapped) space by way of closely measured time, full of unrecognizable people in strange clothing craning their necks, staring at them through handheld telescopes.

Banks's journal records his amazement that the native people glanced up only briefly, then pointedly turned their eyes away from the *Endeavour*, falling back to their fishing as though dismissing a passing phantom irreconcilable with reality. With nothing in common by which to relate to these strangers, diplomatic recognition was effectively denied, though great shock waves from this encounter would soon begin passing through the land. The abrupt appearance of a small English barque under partial sail beneath a blazing Australian sky plainly but silently stated, "The world as we've known it can come to an end."

Equally tragic, those on board the vessel were unable to stretch their minds beyond their European frame of reference to glimpse what was passing before their eyes. Despite the name *Endeavour*, it would take another century and more for these unseeing tourists, and the missionaries and colonists who followed them, to even begin to detect the spiritual depth of the millennia-deep civilization embedded in the land and people they were gazing at so blindly. The advent of the Europeans would set about dismantling the brilliant human-Earth compact finessed in one place for more than sixty thousand years that is the inheritance and gift of indigenous Australia to the world.

Native peoples the world over know what it means to have their sovereignty violated and destroyed. European colonialism has been a disruptive hyperobject for centuries. Only now, everyone on Earth is faced with the hyperobject that is the climate crisis. Hyperobjects by nature are impossible to pin down or localize in space and time, in thought and response; they cut off (with terrible ease) the natural route by which we customarily rouse ourselves to sense and deal with danger.

INVALUABLE PAIN

Caring for what we are losing rightly hurts, but this hurt is invaluable, critical to our instincts to deeply adapt in order to carry us through this crisis. If we look away from all that we are jettisoning from the life raft that is Earth, we jettison our deepest selves. It's impossible not to also confess, "It's my harm." "It's my fault." "It's my responsibility." We thus have a chance to truly discover one another—no longer shying away from reality, but fully inhabiting the complexity of grief, terror, hope, and joy in the present. For the present moment, as always, is our only chance to recognize and confirm our kinship and our continuity with all beings and to reach out to the lives that companion us and support us.

Meanwhile, we're faced with another hyperobject, a vast, virtual obstacle between us and the physical facts of our world. How are we to tame the malignant effects of the half-feral internet and the digital world? It's now always with us, like a fifth limb or second mind, wonderfully well-designed to make us believe we live in a virtual, unreal reality.

Fear, anger, and the desire to shame drive far too much of our engagement with social media. Algorithms keep the alarm and anger level constantly dialled high, while disinformation sets grass fires of fresh outrage to stimy a concerted response. We're trapping ourselves in a new kind of house on fire that is populated by the disembodied presences of countless strangers and bots inspiring both unfounded worry and furious agreement. Disbelief becomes apostasy. Conspiracy has no reverse gear; backing out of an internet rabbit hole is as hard as leaving any extreme cult. Outside its addictive, tightly closed circle of affirmation, you will cease to exist.

The "children" of the Lotus Sutra parable now appear with their heads down, compulsively checking their smartphones, frantically at play in the burning house of our world. This time, not only uninterested in finding the burning exit but infuriated by the suggestion.

SICK BECAUSE THE WHOLE WORLD IS SICK

In the Vimalakirti Sutra, the deeply realized old layman Vimal-akirti is lying sick in his bare, ten-by-ten-foot room. Interestingly, though he is known to be wealthy, his dwelling place is very spare. Vimalakirti's name means "untainted fire." There it is, the fire that runs through all things, untainted by form and emptiness, by yes and no, by right and wrong, by inside and outside. His is the fully human, undivided mind.

The Buddha, meanwhile, is speaking in the mango grove of a famous courtesan, discoursing to many thousands, when he begins to sense that the great layman who lives off at a distance is not well. He asks the gathering of bodhisattvas, one after another, to go and inquire as to why Vimalakirti is sick. And one after another they find important reasons why, sadly, they must refuse the Buddha's request. In the end, it is Manjushri, the bodhisattva of the emptiness wisdom that cannot force distinctions on this undivided reality, who agrees to go to Vimalakirti's modest hut and sickbed, set plainly in the samsaric world of suffering, sickness, old age, and death, to ask the great question in which all medicine begins: "Why are you sick?"

Immediately, all 32,000 bodhisattvas and hangers-on go with him to see what happens, and all prove to be easily accommodated in a ten-by-ten foot hut and seated on huge lion thrones! Practice is like that—you may think you're sitting alone, but the whole world sits with you.

When Manjusri at last gets to ask the great question (very worth asking yourself), Vimalakirti responds, "I am sick because the whole world is sick"—the famous declaration that sits at the heart of the entire sutra. Classically, this sickness is the burning house itself, the unresolved unsatisfactoriness of helpless desire and denial within impermanence—an impotent suffering riddled with lack and loss. However, the humility in

Vimalakirti's refusal to elevate himself above the suffering world is the beautiful and plain self-relinquishment that brings care back into the world. He keeps the whole world attentive company, at ease in the midst of uneasiness, doing the transforming, metabolizing work of healing, of turning suffering into healing medicine.

And don't miss that what comes along implicitly with his unqualified acceptance is this: "I am awake because the whole world is awake!" Again, not one hair's breadth of separation.

ONE TOE IN THE EARTH

The Buddha had earlier revealed to the gathering the true reality of this world. To clarify a despairing question about its broken, falling-down, corruptible appearance, he simply eased one toe into the earth, and to the astonishment of the huge assembly, the dust, confusion, difficulty, and passions of ordinary life suddenly appeared as one true, jeweled radiance, nirvana and samsara indivisible, one fire untainted by difference.

Or as Yunmen would later put it, "The whole Earth is medicine."

The very dust is awake when we are. It comes down to each of us to quell the sickness of separation we ask the Earth to bear. Becoming congruent with suffering is not willed, but suffered in the deepest sense of accepted and borne, transforming into patient, even-minded practice. Fear and joy: one body.

"When everyone is liberated from illness, I will be too," is how Vimalakirti explains the same transforming solidarity with the world of conscious, suffering beings. Healing opens in the place of willingly sharing what we seek to heal. Everyone is sick until no one is. Earth will likewise remain sick until we suffer with her, concede her suffering as our own, and give her our transforming solidarity. Medicine and sickness heal each other when the small human dream of separation suffers its way into conceding how deeply all beings are one body.

THE ORIGINAL NET

"I am sick because the whole world is sick." Vimalakirti's words resonate uncannily with our time of global pandemic, stemming at least in part from our relentless physical and population push into undisturbed ecosystems. Climates changing too fast for human and creaturely adaptation can only further fray ecosystems and accelerate the chance for such novel collisions of species. And each new virus hitches a fossil-fueled ride with ease across the planet in human bodies, while megacities turbocharge its spread.

The term *public health* bundles viral reality into its ethical call to us as individuals inhabiting one shared body that is collectively vulnerable to sickness and collaboratively capable of healing. But only if we inhabit the awareness that your suffering is also my suffering.

The Vedic image of the shimmering net of Indra celebrates every being as one knot in an infinitely extended net, each a multifaceted jewel reflecting every other jewel in the net and the entire net itself. Robert Aitken Roshi (1917–2010) called this holographic vision of reality "the basis of universal health," or reality's fundamental medicine. The tender fact of impermanence is exactly what charges each being with inarguable presence, even as it interweaves all of us into one great network of entirely mutual arising.

Indra's net is visual elaboration of the intelligence of emptiness; call it great compassion. "My illness comes from great compassion," explains Vimalakirti. Nothing about compassion offers blissful refuge from reality. To see through this separate self is to tune in to all the cries of the world. And from that flows ordinary compassion, every spurt of concern for the other, every act of kindness, whatever we can do to help, whenever we can be alert enough. Finding this great compassion and its vast benefit is as simple as the propensity to live larger than this small self.

Like the open-palmed, splayed human handprint, this edgeless sense of being radiates out with relative ease to recognize itself in people, creatures, mountains, rivers, and the great wide Earth, as well as the sun, the moon, and the stars—all of it, all of you, just doing the most natural thing in response. It looks exactly like helping.

Hongzhi, in the exquisite and mysterious poem attributed to him, effectively offers a kind of capping verse centuries after Vimalakirti's koan of sickness transforming into medicine, suffering into realization, and no-self into the ancient ferry that carries all the many beings:

> When, by the side of the ancient ferry,
> The breeze and the moon are cool and pure,
> The dark vessel turns into the glowing world.

Pain and anguish, but also joy, delight, and love, fuel our great human gift of dreaming our way into one another, of coming into the reality of interconnectedness that creates the ancient ferry. All beings ride in it together. There's the glowing world.

Sounds suspiciously like this blue-green planet as well, does it not, plowing through great oceans of space and dark matter?

ONLY FOR YOUR BENEFIT

One time, Dongshan Liangjie (807–869) was down at the creek, silently washing his bowls alongside a young fellow monk, the subtle song of running water and birdsong flowing through them. Both of them were focused intently on their task, yet it was impossible to not be pleasurably aware of the breathing, glistening frog in front of them on a rock in the creek. With shocking suddenness, two birds swooped down, both seizing the frog and tearing it in two as they flew off in opposite directions.

The monk cried out, "Why does it come to this?"

Dongshan replied, "It is only for your benefit, Acharya." The honorific title he bestowed on the monk fully received that human cry of lament and bowed to the wisdom in its pain. But the benefit was left for the monk and us to find us out.

What's really at the core of the cry? Lament torn from our throats throws us beyond ourselves, so the young monk's spontaneous cry was about something greater than his personal concern to be free from the world of suffering. That monk was also ripped in two by two birds. His cry was also for you and me and the unavoidable suffering that's inseparable from our impermanent lives. It's for a world that has come to an unbearable crisis.

And it is also the beneficial cry of open wonder.

Dongshan's "It is only for your benefit" is strange only until we reach beyond "your" to see how to rest the apparent strangeness of this scene in the fullness of not-knowing, which cannot relegate a single thing and banish it from the universe. And the "benefit" he speaks of is no chariot built for one, someone called "me," in which to ascend at last above all earthly cries in order to be relieved of the imperative to respond. It points exactly the opposite way: let this pain willingly endanger your isolated sense of self.

The young monk's anguish affirms that your life is not other than my life. Dongshan's words invite him deeper into that nonseparation, to welcome the responsibility to care that it lays on his life as *benefit*. They don't deny his personal suffering, but charge it with a transforming energy. We're being invited to share suffering's power to wake us up to our interconnected reality.

A formless field of benefaction swims into view—the indivisible nature of all things that gives rise to and sustains the world of every being. The "you" in "your benefit"—who is it? How far do "you" reach? And how might this question refine your response to this time of crisis?

ALL BEINGS, ALL BEINGS

Shoushan Xingnian (926–993) was once asked, "What is a bodhisattva before she becomes a buddha?" "All beings, all beings," was Shoushan's reply.

"How about after she becomes a buddha?" the enquirer wondered. "All beings, all beings," confirmed Shoushan, not moving an inch.

I find this to be a koan for our time of rapidly degrading ecological richness. Two perspectives are under investigation in the monk's heart, but Shoushan warns that to move to separate them would be to break in two.

Before awakening to the fact, our lives are inextricable from all other beings. Not a difficult intellectual leap to make, but how easily it seems we can live in an unchanged way alongside this awareness as a disastrous collapse in biodiversity unfolds. *With* awakening, we find ourselves swimming in a vast, generous, more seamless equality with all beings. *After* awakening, we must consciously bear and embrace what comes along with such a realization.

"All beings" includes you and points decisively to your own heart. And there's nothing generalized here. Each being is utterly unique. There's no such thing as *a* grasshopper in reality until it is *this* grasshopper. Is there really any such thing as *a* human being when each one of us is *this* human being, unique and irreplaceable?

Each living thing returns the grace of your not separating yourself and standing apart. Can we fulfill the wonderfully impossible bodhisattva vow to save all the many beings apart from waking from the dream of separation? In the fullness and grace of reality, it works more like this: All the many living things—you hold yourself toward them, live your life toward them, and they make equally sure of you.

For it's one generosity, extending both ways, impossible to pick apart in the fullness of empty, complete being, or interbeing, as Thich Nhat Hanh called the benefit. Ikkyu put the same flash of light this way:

> It isn't that we're alone or not alone
> whose voice do you want, mine? Yours?

Who is finally who on this Earth? When you're stopped by the call of the mopoke haunting the evening hills, whose voice and whose heart is this? That lovely inseparability and its nameless sense of gratitude is felt anytime we move into full presence in the living world.

Here's Shoushan's "All beings, all beings" as realized by free diver Ross Frylinck in a cold-water marine reserve off Cape Town: A huge school of very beautiful fish swam up and began circling him, unusually friendly and calm around people because they're never hunted. He became totally lost in the enchantment of the meeting until the very cold water at last began to bite through enough to return him to the beach.

"Sitting there in the sun to warm up, the strangest thing happened, [which] hasn't happened since," he wrote. "I heard this voice in my head saying, "Don't be scared." And then these waves of flame just came up through my body and straight out of the top of my head. And it was an awakening. I just knew that I was awake for the first time."

His transformed state lasted days before an ordinary sense of reality slowly resumed, but the experience left him wide-open in a completely different way. "I noticed for the first time how incredibly alive and beautiful the world was," he says. "The rocks, the little rock pools, the animals in the rock pools—everything was alive and not separate."[3]

All yours, a unity impossible to fall out of. Amazed wonder fused with gratitude, the most generous emotion—is there anyone or anything left out of this "benefit"?

THIS VERY BODY

The burning house we live in is of course also this mortal body, toes and all, alive on the thin, barely cooled crust of a molten-cored, ever-changing planet. Our inescapably mortal body, bound to suffer and die, is the only known place of awakening.

Perhaps alone among species we humans suffer a growing apprehension of our own mortality as it snakes through consciousness and bodily awareness like a lit and crackling fuse. And perhaps that's fitting for a species born so utterly helpless, enduring such an extended infancy in which we are completely dependent on the beings around us to insure our survival. Fear of death and fear of lack haunt the consciousness of human beings. A deeply secret mortal fear sits at the back of every breath—probably why it is so infrequently mentioned—maintaining against all odds a sense of living more or less in perpetuity. After all, the pervading, unexamined sense is that we've always been here.

The word *extinction*, now constantly in the air, no doubt primes unexamined fears of personal and even generational mortality. But the deeper jolt is this: with each one of the thousands of species free-falling into the abyss of extinction every day, the creative germ of life-in-tension-with-death that has generated their unique forms is extinguished too, consigning even their mortality to where nothing can ever manifest again.

The skilled ethnographer of Aboriginal peoples, the late Deborah Bird Rose, lamented, "Something is going on here that matters in ways that many of us are not adept at understanding. Perhaps we lack awareness of the beauty of death, and therefore fail to perceive that it is being violated."[4] Calling extinction a "double death," she draws attention to the way species extinction uncouples life from death, undoing death's capacity to turn dying back into the pool of life.

The tragedy of extinction of whole species has many deathly layers to it. If diversity loss piles up at a rate that exceeds a damaged ecosystem's ability to recuperate, a secondary die-off of resilience and renewal sets in for an unknown stretch of time. One falling domino silently topples another ten. When the rate of extinctions begins to exceed the rate of new species appearing, we can say that the death of evolution itself is happening in that place and will continue for an unknowable duration.

This vast unraveling erases from memory the effort of generations of beings to live and successfully pass on life, just as if that great effort had never existed either, curtailing not only a future for a unique species but also wiping away the provenance of all past lives, which now count for nothing. A vast net of living relationships, entrusted to us across the unbroken reach of generations, has begun to fray. Will we mindlessly allow it to be laid waste?

Species have become extinct countless times in the recorded life on Earth, but never before as the result of one species consciously persisting with choices that so clearly tear unnumbered other life-forms down. Even the significance of your own deeply personal death begins to wither as the great shimmering web of relationships starts to go dark, dull, and dead. The burning house we must admit to our conscious awareness and save from the flames is far more than just a viable world for human beings; biodiversity collapse is the tragedy of our times. The Earth household is formed by all life. Our mourning for a safe future must not be wasted but turned to praise and defence of the infinite value of "all beings, all beings."

Your own waking up is for them or else it is not a waking up at all.

A profound refashioning of the human heart begins here. Dependent coarising, the fundamental understanding of early Buddhism, takes root in the awakening of emptiness wisdom and blossoms into an ecologically based awareness of the creative force and flow of all beings within an alive reality. Realizing all beings as one body of being inseparable from your own delivers a universal ethos of mutual reliance and mutual care. It's as natural and inarguable as wind moving and seeds blowing, waves toppling and salt hissing. Nothing in the moving world can be taken apart.

The pain of seeing with what ignorant ease we desecrate this formless, tenderly alive reality grows sharper, not easier, with this realization. But this pain is valuable for the fiercely protective feelings it brings to life. Meanwhile, the fundamental conditions for our flourishing along with all other living beings remain starkly simple and nonnegotiable: Exact levels of oxygen. Fresh, clean water. Fresh, clean food. Fresh, clean air. A place to shelter. The companionship of other beings.

And for human beings, one extra, critically important, simple, nonnegotiable condition: that we awaken to how completely the lives of all the other beings and the whole sentient Earth is also our own life, our own immediate flourishing, and, if ignored, our own great undoing.

RIPENESS IS ALL

The water that comprises so much of your body's cells is flowing through them on a beginningless journey—as snowmelt a thousand miles away three weeks ago, as a thunderstorm last night, as this sip of water now. And tomorrow or soon after, all this becomes ocean. The cells themselves also flow through, forming and dying within an overall homeostasis that is the living pattern of free interchange called a body.

"Ripeness is all," as Edgar says to the blind, failing Gloucester in Shakespeare's great tragedy *King Lear*. "Men must endure their going hence, even as their coming hither." And yet even in our going hence is our coming hither, arriving in every moment.

What is our enduring substance? What is there to cling to in this empty, alive ripeness of passing through? And at exactly the same time, our choices and actions manifest and shape the way things can flow, far beyond where knowing can reach and direct. Ripeness is present in the vulnerability of every human being in Earth's accepting embrace, as is the split-open ripeness of the Japanese poet Issa's cry of protest, "And yet! And yet." This ripeness is a constant healing into impermanence.

To exercise not-knowing is to favor wonder over fear or mistrust, so that when confronted by someone's harsh words or actions, the ripe response wants to sound the genuine pain of the other without first approving or dismissing their beliefs. Ripeness is acceptance of the inherently precarious nature of this very moment, for every moment is the universe at its zenith and in the moment of its creation. Live according to this richer state of being here, and it welcomes you. It's our true home.

What does it take to become receptive to what is trying to be heard, seen, born, and actualized in a fluctuating and deteriorating world? Its agenda is unwritten, and we are always tasked with divining and taking direction from its most subtle signs.

Hongzhi, in a verse in *The Book of Equanimity*, gives a clue about the generosity of spirit the Earth is trying to summon: "Those who know the heart bring it forth—don't haggle." And what is there, finally, to haggle with? We learn in another line from the same verse that there is "Nothing to stand on, no place to fall." Trust the fearlessness of this—good medicine to keep handy for an easily panicked heart. It defends the great collective benefit that is usually more generous than we can manage to embody. Not-knowing sees the impulse to help, save, and share to be as natural and unqualified as self-nature.

Ripeness is you and me at our most extended reach, relaxed in the shared tenderness of being here. Such ripeness sees past right and wrong, good and bad, you and me, resolving what is divided back into the wide intelligence of emptiness. In seventh-century China, the words of the famous Sixth Ancestor, Huineng, lit up the same idea: "Emptiness includes the sun, moon, stars, and planets, the great Earth, mountains and rivers, all trees and grasses, bad people and good people, bad things and good things, heaven and hell; they are all in the midst of emptiness. The emptiness of human nature is also like this."

The emptiness of human nature is also like this. Huineng's final benediction, like every blessing, is also his challenge to our compulsive passions and tricky nature, to the frequent fog of being human. The emptiness of bad people and good people, bad things and good things, heaven and hell are much harder to spot for a human being than the blameless emptiness of wind blowing through trees or drops of rain spreading in widening, intersecting circles in a pool of water.

But how does the emptiness of our complex human nature come to our rescue and open the way in the midst of the burning house and failing health of a moment like the one we're in?

CODA: IS THERE ONE WHO IS NOT SICK?

"Medicine and sickness heal each other. The whole Earth is medicine." Yunmen's words challenge every move of the divided, opposed, manipulative mind. We're all together in the burning house of being, and inseparable from each other and the Earth.

In Case 94 of *The Book of Equanimity* we find the great Tang dynasty master Dongshan once more, this time unwell, possibly dying. Even so, a monk with some questions comes by to see him.

"Your Reverence is unwell. Is there someone, after all, who is not sick?" he wonders. He's not asking about someone other than the one lying sick before him, but when Dongshan confirms, "There is," then who or what is the "someone" in question?

"Does the one who is not sick nurse Your Reverence?" wonders the monk.

"This old monk is properly nursing that one," replies Dongshan, inviting the monk to share his own attentive freedom within conditions.

The monk, grasping what Dongshan has said, finally asks the question that I suspect brought him to the sick room of his teacher in the first place: "How is it when Your Reverence nurses him?"

"Then the old monk does not see that there is any sickness at all," says Dongshan, perhaps reaching shakily for a sip of water as he does so.

Here we find Dongshan fully congruent with actual conditions, beyond better or worse. Nothing is missing even in his fast-weakening state.

Somewhere on the path to falling awake, practice ceases being something you *do*. You notice it has become something you *are*, just a natural kind of homage to this life. And what you are at this most fundamental level does not disparage the persistent sense of a separate self, nor the falling away of life into death, any more than fire refuses the twig on which it burns. The moment the walls of fear in the mind come down, this open state of consciousness verifies the true nature of reality, with nothing filtered out and no filtering out of ourselves.

Even so, a place of no sickness at all? On a planet stampeding toward ruin? Where is that free, open place of responding? How does the one who is not sick, mind free in emptiness, not seeing any sickness at all, "properly nurse" the startled reactions of our jumpy human heart?

cupped in weathered hands his daughter's smile

火

5

THE LOTUS IN THE MIDST OF FLAME

Without leaving the demon world, enter the Buddha world.
—ZEN CAPPING PHRASE

Question: What is the path beyond mistakes?
Dogen: Do not leave this place abruptly.

Scene on a packed train full of people, in the early days of the COVID-19 pandemic: A woman, not wearing a mask, coughed loudly, pointedly not covering her mouth. The man standing next to her in direct range of her cough reacted angrily, demanding, "Why aren't you wearing a mask like everyone else?" The woman immediately turned and coughed aggressively in exaggerated fashion right into his dismayed face. An entire train car full of people became incensed, fury building against the woman, who seemed now to be gleefully relishing the anger she was arousing.

But then another man, small child in tow, eased his way up to her through the crowded train. Very gently touching her arm, he asked calmly but firmly, "Are you *right*?"

She looked him in the eyes, slightly shocked, yet visibly more coherent, and immediately began making her way to the doors to get off at the next station. No accusing eyes were directed at her as she pushed her way through. Quieted and relieved by that tiny intervention, everyone on the train just looked away, giving her space.

The nonpartisan care in the touch and words "Are you *right?*" quelled the panicked spite and rage in the woman and healed the outrage of an entire train car, leaving everyone a little more emotionally informed.

In this path beyond mistake, the man did not "leave this place abruptly." His tone was calm, his words not accusatory, yet they conveyed just enough unsticky concern—as in, "Are you all right?"—while checking her behavior as being evidently *not* right in every obvious way. Skillfully noncoercive, he left things in the woman's own mind to be examined by her—a question, not a finding, a very ripe response, right on the point of the moment. She was safely shifted into a neutral place, where she was personally met, not despised, and not opposed in any way that could fuel more defensive anger. He just enabled her to find her own next move, her own way home, while nudging the other people on the train onto the same path in the process.

SUCH QUARRELS

That woman's behavior looked to me like rabid fear and frantic denial of a force that the world cannot control. Whether runaway climate collapse or unstoppable COVID-19, this kind of fear easily turns into aggressive defensiveness. The one border that can be policed and controlled becomes the skin that will never permit the reality of a virus to penetrate it, the sovereign self that will never permit limitations to be placed on it, the national border that will never permit fleeing people to cross it, and so forth. In her eyes she was taking a stand against a tsunami of uncontrollable forces that would strip her of all power to exert agency.

It takes courage to dare to realize that control is inseparable from fear, and that anger and hatred often mask a deeply wounded love. And yet, "The softest thing on Earth overtakes the hardest thing on Earth," as the Tao Te Ching puts it.

In light of this great, mixed world, a monk came to Zhaozhou, wondering, "Among the ten thousand things, which is the most solid?"

Zhaozhou replies, "When we curse at each other, that we can go on flapping our lips. When we spit at each other, that we can have our saliva flow out."

Zhaozhou is marveling at the wonderful way that hatred discloses the clearest glimpse of what is most solid: the strongly confronted self. And can't you hear in his wonder the tender delicacy of a sentient world that stands so wide open to the violence of our ignorant abuse? As the great Japanese poet Kobayashi Issa (1763–1828) writes,

> In the dewdrop
> of this dewdrop world ~
> such quarrels

"Such quarrels!" From the moment a smartphone was in almost every human hand, it seems the human id was granted a license to publish. How vividly Zhaozhou portrays the self-convinced and fortified sense of self! Spit flying, lips flapping, whether in heated, face-to-face encounters or in the brutalizing dreamscape that is social media, highly charged "knowing" redoubles itself in every curse, threat, and insult.

Meanwhile, the world burns.

HAZY MOON

Demented, human-created systems like those now devouring the life of the Earth need to come apart so we can discover the true ground of being here where we are. The human being safely tucked into the small self needs to fall away freely in order to find the original, unimpeded self that is shared with all beings. There is a consonance between these two matters that compels close attention, and rightfully so, because self-relinquishment opens a wider perspective at every point.

But of course it's a joy tinged with grief that learns to face this grievously mixed world as it is. Zen praises the value of the "hazy moon of enlightenment" that not merely tolerates but embraces the crazed, sad, dreamy, fogged, painful faces of humanity. Joy and grief are intimates; both live at the ground level of the passions held in the human heart.

A powerful feeling is more like a wave than a state of being. Not only is it passing through in a compelling form, it sometimes breaks over everything around it on its tumultuous way, and like any wave it contains a multitude of elements—stingers, long strands of seaweed, blinding swirls of sand, stray fish, and plastic flotsam, jetsam, and particles of untraceable matter—as well as limitless ocean and life-giving energy. Then recedes.

Take a feeling of deep anger: what is actually coming along with its compulsive groundswell of hot or cold energy? If you take your time with it, letting it ebb and flow through you, you might find that sadness is its deepest tone. The sadness may have layers of fear in it, such as fear for the ones you love and the places you love. Or it may secrete the fear of finding what you are not able to love enough. Inside this may lie the fundamental collecting point of grief—that nothing lasts, bodies grow old and feeble, and we wound one another and can't undo that. We do harm to what is blameless and defend what is indefensible, and at the very foundation of all of this breaking energy lies an unmoving ground, a bedrock of fundamental joy and love that may take great, persistent endurance to finally reach and confirm. Climate grief, unexamined, disables and destroys our ability to respond. But lived into with an open awareness of its complexity, such grief can release latent creative energy to flow freely. Waves of grief, waves of anger, waves of sorrow—each carry with them an offer of self-relinquishment, and all that opens from there. Xuedou says, "The dragon's jewel is found in every wave; looking for the moon, it is found in this wave, in that wave." This is the radical inclusiveness of Zen, which throws up a great, life-restoring koan in the face of archaic forms of Buddhism that would cut off the passions as "unwholesome" and life as worthy only of permanent escape.

THE RED THREAD OF ZEN

To be completely purified of the messy human condition is an old, completely understandable human dream. It wistfully lodges in us despite the raw evidence of a perpetually unfinished universe that is never finished with us. In such a universe as this, each thing is complete and present in its own right, beyond improvement. The perfection dream conducts a puritanical quarrel with the passing-through nature of all things and all beings. The dream generates astonishing and ruinous conflicts in the human world and further dampens the sputtering fire of life on earth.

Every attempt to escape the emotional messiness of our condition misses an opportunity and creates a prison, whereas accepting what is holds open a wide, nonjudging embrace of our humanity as the place (the only place) where real awakening begins. Zen is distinctive in venerating the mysterious unbreakable thread that connects vast emptiness with this thoroughly mammalian human embodiment. Our blood, passions, suffering, and all that comes with it—the hazy, ordinary human world—warms and values emptiness. This mortal body, this unpredictable life, is the sole ground of liberation. And one koan above all venerates this.

From Songyuan Chongyue's (1139–1209) "Three Turning Words" comes a deceptively simple question: "Why are perfectly accomplished saints and bodhisattvas still attached to the red thread?"

Sometimes "red thread" is translated as "vermilion thread," since in old China courtesans were obliged to dye their underwear an intense vermilion. The immediate connotations of "the red thread" are sexual passion, lust, and love. But it would be mistake to see Songyuan's "Why?" as voicing regret for the difficulty of breaking free of such powerful bonds. Instead, this "Why" breaks us open into to the idea that awake human beings cannot, should not, indeed must not seek to cut themselves free of this messy yet marvelous red thread. And certainly not on a planet like this one, for this bloodred koan offers an exquisitely human lifeline from the Earth and back to the Earth, heightening each person's life while constantly healing us back into our original, empty wholeness.

The elemental fact of mammalian biology is the umbilical cord that links the fetal and maternal bodies, confirmed in every human body by the presence of the belly button. The unconditional caring in the mother that the newborn creates by the sheer helplessness of its compelling presence comes along, bringing with it blood, lineage, family trees, the Tree of Life, and the great mix of passions born in each vulnerable human life, together with the strong demands those passions make on our awareness and understanding.

This red thread of unbreakable interconnectedness is sometimes called "the line of tears," evoking the compassion born of suffering as well as our innate inability to *not* hear the cries of the world, no matter how hard we work to drown them out with mental noise.

And so the red thread compels our liberating and imaginative embrace of the whole of life, including its pain and darkness and our own personal extinction. Its vast, ever-opening "Why?" invites the deepest inquiry into the nature of humanness and personhood, as well as the struggle to fully bring who we really are forward to meet the immediacy of the planetary crisis.

The red thread of alive interconnectedness that cannot be cut admits the whole of what we are as all-too-human beings, as well as the loud and painfully stifled cries of a world in crisis, into the intimacy of not-knowing—its tender, skin-to-skin closeness and its greathearted roominess. It is the human mind opening to all that is.

This is the lotus in the midst of flame.

THESE CRIES ARE FOR ALL BEINGS

Avalokitesvara, also known as Guanyin (Kuan Yin), the bodhisattva of compassion, hears all the cries of the world. This is an unqualified attention that is the natural state of openness, of no-self.

The cry of the bodhisattva now rings with undertones of grief for the state of the world. Consider the impossible grief of watching the Great Barrier Reef, the largest single organism on Earth, visible even from space—an entire world of its own that shocks the imagination back into full life—transform before our appalled eyes into a graveyard of bleached coral in water that is insistently growing too warm and acidic to allow for recovery. Such sorrow gnaws at the hearts of millions and brings scientists to tears in front of their students.

In the record of Zhaozhou is mentioned a woman whose exceptional clarity attracted many Zen students. When her beloved granddaughter died, she wept openly and loudly in front of everyone. People were shocked.

"A master like you, and you weep? Impermanence is just impermanence, why mourn like this?"

She scolded them soundly, saying, "Of course I weep! These cries are for all beings. Listen, listen!"

Later, Zhaozhou heard about this controversial outbreak and simply asked, "How can anyone lose by crying out?" Crying out with justifiable pain and grief is not only appropriate, it has the power to awaken us.

Zazen is like Guanyin's deep listening; we receive without resistance and without straining. It does not and cannot hold against the weeping of a heartbroken grandmother, the cries of refugees in the water, the bellowing of cows for their calves taken from them, the silent shriek of trees desiccated by drought. The cries that are heard are indeed cries for all beings, every lament highly particular and universally resonant. Each cry saves those who cry out, and each rescues those who are pierced by the cries from self-imposed exile. A heartfelt cry, entire with your whole being, draws caring to the surface and rouses to life the mutual benefit shared among all beings. When you cry out with your whole body and mind, is there any self at all?

How can anyone lose by being one with what is, without resistance? Sickness working as medicine, grief working as healing, the lotus blooming inseparable from the flame.

On another occasion, previously mentioned in passing, old Zhaozhou was approached by a questioner—not a monk this time, but again a woman in the depths of grief for a lost grandchild. "What is *this?*" she asks him. At that moment, her question was no standard opening to draw a master's clarifying response about the nature of reality. It was that, of course, but elevated into the untrammeled cry of "*Why*?" from the heart of all anguish, all despair, all helpless grief.

Zhaozhou responds, "The heart of the one who asks."

There it is! Our grief cuts through to the heart of what is. At the same time his words completely resound with the woman's anguish for the impossible loss of her grandchild—not looking at it, but moved and moving with it. Whose heart is whose? The one who knows cannot be found and cannot divide acceptance from the very human cry of protest.

AND YET

Until we can hear the cries of the world and let them pierce through to the undivided place in ourselves, we can't realize the cries of the world and the angry groaning of the Earth as our own.

Until then, we're prone to be ghosts to ourselves and to one another, ghosts to the Earth. A cry completely heard can shatter the dream of any gap between self and human or creaturely others, self and the living Earth. Intimacy appears, all beings are close, and the way is very wide.

The way opens in the intelligence of being with anguish and distress, and we wake up in the act of moving to lessen suffering or to regenerate what has been desecrated. Where else could it arise in a world ablaze with exigency? Life is uncertain. Being alive is trouble. It hurts. The wind stings, and even the water hurts when it hits us hard. Even joy hurts, for nothing is left out of it. It is (at the very bottom) okay. Difficulty is the métier, the genius and the raw material of transformation. In any moment of full attention there is no way we can escape the fire. The lotus in the flames manifests in not seeking to escape what is. What we need to find to save the Earth from ourselves will be found in those flames.

It was a fresh smallpox outbreak that carried away Issa's beloved two-year-old daughter, rending his heart:

The world of dew
is the world of dew.
And yet! And yet

His poem for her is a cry that is equally an acceptance of this world of loss and a profoundly human protest. He bows completely to that fact, and he howls with unrefused grief.

John Tarrant remarked that those two words, "And yet," form the great gate of the Mahayana. Wider than wide-open, it accepts all offers, turning away nothing. Emptiness runs as fully through Issa's measured acceptance that all things pass away as swiftly as the morning dew in the sunlight, as it does through his heartbroken gasp, wrung from him by impossible grief.

There's no pious foreclosure here, no refusal or shamed or angry withdrawal from any part of the pain of living. Instead, we have full consent to the empty nature of difficult emotions—which is to hold lamentation and joy not separate, but healing into each other. And neither permits retreat. The way opens exactly here.

Every koan points back to the heart and in doing so, confirms, in one light, then another, the value of how our lives cry out. And every awakening glimpse confirms the intimacy of human pain with an unbounded heart-mind. They open to each other; like sickness and medicine, they mutually resolve.

No retreat from this is exactly what opens the way.

NOT-TWO

Two crossed swords, neither permitting retreat,
Dextrously wielded, like the lotus in the midst of fire,
Thus you resolve from your heart to ascend the heavens.

—DONGSHAN

Dongshan's fiery image of a very alive, engaged quality of mind within the chafe of the conditions of life on Earth comes in the fourth part of his ten-part poem "The Five Ranks." His verse affords five angles of view of the field of awakening, offered in each of two modes.

"Two crossed swords" meet in the equipoise of push and counterpush: there's your life, each ordinary and extraordinary moment of it—not just lotus exactly meeting fire, but impermanence saturated with the eternal, relative world inseparable from the absolute, this very self exactly meeting no-self. Birth and death in every breath. There's no retreat possible from the not-two nature of what you are and what is, like it or not, awake to it or not.

To "dextrously wield" this not-two nature of reality is a humble matter, calling on you to remain as congruent as humanly possible with exactly what is happening, exactly what calls out to your hands and eyes. Love can't remain a noun but must be realized as a verb. What calls out for your love that, if ignored, will slowly asphyxiate your life?

Nothing permits retreat. Christopher Robin, the close friend of Winnie-the-Pooh, roundly declared he liked all kinds of weather as long as he was out in it. The path invites us to walk in wind and rain and fire and pandemic, and in all the indigestible feelings of dissonance and doubtfulness that compounds fear, under the pressure of an unavoidable global crisis complicated by the constant choices of our immediate life circumstances.

Should I change my job to something that coheres with my fear for the world? Should I drive instead of fly, walk instead of drive? Should I challenge the intolerable absurdity of my coworkers' dismissal of the reality of climate change and destroy the friendliness in the office? How do I forgive myself for managing to live much of the time remote from the fact of this huge planetary tragedy from which I cannot extricate myself? How can we not shrink prematurely from the pain of our circumstances or the friction of one another, remaining steady in meeting the powerful feelings that arise as we walk the way from the dark before conception to the final "I don't know," which is death?

The way itself—so mixed and contentiously human. Other people are the path. After all, who else but the other is there to make sure that we discover how to be with uncomfortable feelings, to see past our self-confirming knowing and projections? Who else to let us know we are beloved and to disclose the hardest task of love—to loosen the grip maintained by this self.

In the fullness and grace of reality it works like this: All the many living beings—hold yourself toward them, live your life toward them, and they make sure of you. They teach by example, without even lifting a finger, how life yields to suffering, old age, sickness, and death.

No one is left out of this universal grace of being, that hurts us into tenderness.

THE OPEN RESPONSE

When you look closely, there is nothing that stands alone, immaculate, untouched. Our completeness affirms and rests in an overlapping and interwoven state of being. All other beings also comprise us. No wonder there's no awakening separate from an awake universe. Each thing is holy and reflects the mysterious and evolving whole while enjoying and suffering the beautiful lunacy of its mixed, broken-open state. Zazen returns us incessantly to "just as it is," our true home, and koans pry open the treasure in that incessant return.

The net of Indra can't sort anything out from anything else: each singular jewel across the net's infinite array of knots cannot help but reflect, in each of its facets, every other being or thing. We interpenetrate. We "inter-are." Emptiness kindly includes our old, understandable dream of a separate self, but equally and blamelessly together with a self that has fallen into awakening from that very strange human dream and from all the damage that it has wrought.

Of course, the more familiar you will gradually resume the center stage of consciousness needed to navigate a complex human world, but practice does not let you ever entirely forget the undivided reality you've glimpsed. And in that glimpse, you've felt it; and in that feeling, you've confirmed it. What comes so very naturally can never be faked. You can't forget your true self anymore than an animal can misplace what it is and how to be itself, for when you see yourself clearly in the other, the whole world is radically revised in that seeing. It has found out how to be whole in you again.

Torei Zenji (1621–1692) was student and dharma heir of Hakuin Ekaku, the great renovator of Japanese koan Zen. In his "Bodhisattva's Vow," Torei humbly takes up the courage of offering a nonviolent, open response, even in the face of someone who persecutes us with abusive language—just as we have been persecuting and abusing the Earth and flinging abuse at the perceived wrongdoers:

> All the more, we can be especially sympathetic
> and affectionate with foolish people,
> particularly with someone who becomes a sworn enemy
> and persecutes us with abusive language.
> That very abuse conveys the Buddha's loving-kindness.
> It is a compassionate device to liberate us entirely
> from the mean-spirited delusions we have built up
> with our wrongful actions from the beginningless past.
> With our open response to such abuse
> we completely relinquish ourselves,
> and the most profound and pure faith arises.[1]

The "open response" is the move that does not retaliate for the suffering it perceives mirrored in the abuse, yet stands its ground, empty of judgment. Such a response opens a "pure," untrammelled energy of engagement, with the sense of self lying low or completely given away in opening the way.

In Torei Zenji's awake, open response, nothing is being actively opposed to anything else. Medicine and sickness are healed into each other, meeting in the middle. Insult or abuse is not taken up as insult or abuse, but accepted in the way the song of that caroling magpie is accepted, straight to the heart held clear of preferences. Warbling magpie or harsh words: either way, it listens in the place that is *open*.

"Do not find fault with the present moment," offers Keizan, testing this matter.

It's a mild-looking koan, huge in its ask. Faultfinding is easy, as easy as reacting and missing the moment completely, as easy as never really arriving here where we are, which is the only place where any congruent response ever began.

The practice of active, transformative not-knowing is indeed a humbling business. *Humble*—a beautiful word that not only brings with it humility and awareness of how we humiliate the Earth with our indifference but also returns us to the Earth herself, for *humus*, the root of *humble*, is another word for earth, soil, the ancestral ground we walk on. What good luck to find it is also the root of *humor!*

This open response, so thoroughly earthy and at home— when we manage to find it, we're home.

IS IT SO?

In early adulthood, Hakuin lived for a time as a mendicant monk in a hut on the edge of a fishing village. He did his alms rounds, and in return the neighborhood appreciated having a practicing monk nearby, freeing everyone to feel a little pious while getting on with worldly business.

One day, suddenly and shockingly, he heard a loud, angry knocking on his door. He opened it to find a furious woman standing alongside her shamefaced daughter, thrusting forth a newborn baby, saying, "You deceiving monk, she's told us everything! Here, you take the baby!"

Hakuin did not know this woman or her daughter. Accused of breaking his vows and merely masquerading as a monk, what could he do? He reached out and accepted the baby, saying simply, "Ah, is it so?"

The next days, weeks, and months were very difficult. A mendicant monk carrying both a baby and a begging bowl is not met with welcome. And a newborn baby rivets all attention to its needs in a way that quickly becomes a form of love too complete to even recognize as either love or not love. The baby makes sure of this, the bond that creates both lives.

Almost inevitably, but equally suddenly, there was another loud knocking on the door of Hakuin's hut. Holding the baby, he opened it to find the furious woman once more with her shamefaced daughter.

"She's told us everything," said the woman. "It was the boy down in the fish market. Give us back the baby!"

And with mixed feelings he handed that tiny and now beloved baby back across the doorway into the arms of the angry woman, saying simply, "Ah, is it so?"

Hakuin's equal embrace of two such difficult—and different—moments is a kindness deeper than anything that could be thought out. Not-knowing is most intimate, not a hair's breadth off of what is happening or who stands in front of you. But it is full of feeling.

Notice, too, the words that come with the outbreath of "Ah" as he utters the phrase common in Japanese, "Sōdesu ka?" or "Ah yes, isn't it so?" thereby relaxing into what has become understood to be necessary and of some use. There is no move to find responsibility lying elsewhere, a place that shows up on no map. It's natural to look for satisfaction or safety outside of where, what is, right now, but of course it's where everything actually is, discovering through you what it wants.

"Is it so?" remains a question, not a finding. It doesn't hold a view, offer irony, or imply ambivalence. Not-knowing withholds judgment and blame. Hakuin's response was an offer equally of friendliness toward himself, the woman, the girl, the baby, and the whole village—all while things kept on evolving, as is their way. Equanimity is the strong form of self-containment, hard to tell from love. It neither accepts nor rejects insult or condemnation, and its open form of response is not subservient to fear or to demands but impartially interested in discovery. What is really happening, what is needed, what bears the weight of truth? These are the kinds of discoveries that self-protective fear, anger or denial preemptively shut down.

Emergencies can wake up the keenest and most sustained attention to what is needed. How can we allow that attention to be as unrushed and unforced as Hakuin's "Is it so?" His question slows the confronted sense of "It is so!" down to a navigable speed. Attention is not seized by what might happen, but stays intent on finding the opening through line.

A BAT OUT OF HELL

A monk asks Zhaozhou, "Do enlightened teachers ever fall into hell?" Zhaozhou immediately replies, "I'll be the first to go there!" Or in another translation, "They're the first to go there!"

Astonished, the monk protests, "But you're an enlightened teacher! Why would you fall into hell?"

Zhaozhou replies, "If I didn't fall into hell, how could I help you?"

One time when driving at dawn to a weeklong sesshin north of Sydney, I turned from a minor road onto a wide and empty four-lane highway. Well, almost entirely empty: in the far distance a dark motorcycle quickly appeared coming at an extraordinary speed. It seemed I had made the grievous error of turning into the lane he was traveling in. He drew up fast beside me, gesturing furiously about something, his face unreadable behind the black visor on his helmet as we approached a red light. When I stopped at the light, he leapt off his bike and reached through the window I wound down to hear his complaint and immediately wrapped both hands tightly round my throat.

Perhaps I was already in the mind of sesshin, for I didn't freeze and felt no fear, only an oddly calm concern for him. Having ridden motorcycles myself, I knew the fear of being invisible to motorists, so his rage also felt somewhat reasonable, if out of place on a wide and almost completely empty dawn road.

When I failed to react as required, he abruptly let go, rage collapsing into more conventional displays of shouted abuse and a show of kicking the tires of my car. After that, as the light turned green, he remounted his huge black motorcycle and shot away at frightening speed, a demonic, dark dot appearing and disappearing over the next few rises of the road in a vanishing roar.

My heart went with him. He did not feel like a human being who cared to live for long.

If my heart can't fall with yours into hell, if I can't recognize and meet your suffering from my own experience of hatred and ill will, we can't help even ourselves let alone be of some use in aiding a sick planet. The willing, nonjudging, empathic fall into hell can find no barrier. Wonder, replacing judgment, returns to its place as the consecration of the world.

It's hard to find a character condemned in a Chekhov story. Chekhov's easy, frank interest in every human being and each encounter in his stories renders them in pellucid clarity. Their every flaw becomes plain to the reader while the author, with great delicacy, leaves all judgment unspoken. A deeply informing, companionable light is refracted off the exacting details of each situation. Nothing's wasted if it's human. The advice to writers that is frequently attributed to him, though probably derived from related comments in a letter to his brother, is surely borne out in his stories' tender curiosity toward human complexity: "Don't tell me the moon is shining; show me the glint of light on broken glass."

Every mistake and flaw of the world, even difficult emotions or compulsive passions, refracts the moonlight of awake mind. Emotions easily become powerful, difficult, and destructive, which is to say valuable chances to find the nonreactive, undefended response congruent with what is needed—provided we're not overpowered by them.

And remember, *xing*, meaning "practice," is also "to act in concert with." You and me and the world, right where we are, one body of feeling, acting together. To the degree that it does not recognize any gap between the self and the other, such helping in hell is unflustered. And being "the first to go there" is the simple immediacy of what happens in no time at all. Me and you, undivided.

No one pretends it is not demanding work to fall with open eyes into hellish feelings. The hell of hot anger can really be the fear of loss of control, or it can be to fiercely protest the fact of expectations burning up right in front of our eyes. It can hold itself down in depression and unnameable sadness for the lost beauty and balance of the living Earth, which robs us of all energy and agency and can find no reliable future free of any hellish cast.

Zhaozhou's willingness to meet the hell of another being's suffering state of mind has several aspects. The no-self alive in his not-knowing recognizes himself in the other and meets their "compulsive passions" with no condemnation at the ready. "Two crossed swords, neither permitting retreat" are alive in his statement of complete readiness: "I'll be the first to go there." He's already there to meet you in hell—no-gap—which is equally coming to meet himself.

And so the intelligence won from never abruptly leaving the instructive hell of his own mistakes and "compulsive passions" opens the way to "If I didn't fall into hell, how could I help you?"

A longtime student of Zen once recounted how he moved through a deeply confronting moment. People were anxiously trying to avoid all possible contact with a huge, infuriated man shouting semi-incoherent obscenities in the street as they made their way along the crowded sidewalk. A Black man, he was horrifying everyone by freely bestowing the N word on each person forced to pass him—that humanity-erasing curse word that must no longer be hurled at Black people. When it came his turn to receive the curse, he found himself stopping and quietly meeting the gaze of the enraged man, and simply saying, "Thank you."

In that "Thank you," medicine and sickness healed into each other, and a moment of peace descended on that sidewalk, about as long as forever. And then the man recommenced his impassioned work of uttering his harsh cries to all beings.

Without leaving the demon world, walk and meet the other, who is not other than this self, in the Buddha world.

TEACHING DEMONS TO SIT

In skillful hands, "lotus in the fire" becomes "the fire is the lotus."

Zhaozhou famously refused to reject the passions of being human and would question even the proviso of drawing nearer or farther away from them, putting an end to any whiff of separation. Instead, he walked right up to them in the interested and nonpartisan spirit of "I choose!"

He startled people completely by saying, "Buddha is compulsive passions, compulsive passions are Buddha."

Hearing him say this, a monk asked, perhaps nervously, "In whom does Buddha cause passion?" If the Buddha is compulsive passions, what hope is there for a monk seeking equanimity and cool relief from them?

Zhaozhou reassured him, "Buddha causes passions in all of us." Undeterred, the monk pressed on with his self-improvement project, asking, "How should we get rid of them?"

And so Zhaozhou left him with no escape from the unruly passions and the desperate need to get free of them, while setting the monk on a lifetime path of wonder and inquiry that might relieve him of the sense of a separate self. He replied, "Why should we get rid of them?"

Here it is again—the challenge to turn toward what is happening and closely attend to it, noticing but not judging. This is the metabolic process of sickness healing into medicine. Not trying to abandon an uncomfortable feeling abruptly, how is this strong, disruptive, or compulsive feeling moving and settling in your body? How does it feel up close? Staying with it, letting the uppermost wave of feeling slowly disclose what's there a little way down from it, and then below that, and then all the way down at the level where almost nothing is moving at all, what intelligence is this strong, mixed wave of feeling trying to raise to recognition at the deepest level? What does it need you to know about what is needed right now right where you are?

Moment by moment, feelings never stop flowing in some form, bearing an intelligence that needs to be noticed and refined. Bodhicitta, that human yearning to wake up, is itself a fire of impassioned feeling being shaped by loving, rigorous inquiry. Realization is a blaze of vast and equal awareness, a profoundly coherent ecstasy. Why should we get rid of it?

Compulsive passions are Buddha: colliding with them, recognizing them clearly, using them fully, they open the way of awakening. But also, Buddha is compulsive passions: the awakened state initiates new, more exacting domains of discovery about itself. Every day on this side of the grave, the path to awakening is strewn with bright and solemn feelings, emotional and physical pain barriers, and one lucky chance after another to see more deeply into this mysterious self and the generosity of equanimity. Or as Gary Snyder sums it up, "Buddhism offers demons a hand and then tries to teach them to sit."[2] Which of course is to say the path appears in our willingness to let them teach *us* to sit. Zhaozhou's "If I did not fall into hell, how could I help you?" has no trace in it of sarcasm. It merely lays out the path of Zen's acceptance of the great schemozzle that is being a human being—embodied, mortal, and very alive and subject to human passions. Such open acceptance asks of us all that we are. It asks of us that we don't mistake the delicate lotus of awakened mind as any kind of a holdout from the transforming fire of suffering.

Zen says the lotus blooms brightest when sought in the fire of our mortality, our suffering, and our blundering mistakes—the entire blaze of impassioned feelings. Even better, it blooms as the seamless fire, as one unqualified but discerning embrace beyond good or bad.

NO FIRE, NO LOTUS

With no suffering there would be no profound invitation to see through to our original nature, which is also the original nature of all the beings we will ever encounter. Zen koans dissolve the dream of a landlocked self and draws us into intimacy with all beings. Realization ripens by entering this mixed world of imperfect beings. Until then, it is a tasteless fruit.

The testing practice of becoming the lotus in the flame stretches us to our furthest reach in sharing the tenderness, benefit, joy, depth, pain, suffering, care, and the sheer poetry of *being* itself—even, and perhaps especially, under the threat of danger. The flame in the lotus is radical acceptance. When you can hear in your own heartbeat the beating of other hearts, then each instance of life, once unsorted as to whether good or bad, difficult or easy, is just one valuable offer after another.

I once sat in a small circle of meditators bearing silent witness as part of a large, intense protest against a huge arms expo being held in the national capital. As delegates to the expo drew up in chauffeur-driven cars, they were greeted by a barrage of screams of "scumbags, scumbags, scumbags!" Meanwhile, we sat in zazen, letting our meditation equalize the light rain falling on our hats and shoulders, the screaming in our ears, the drumming and the chanting, and the occasional squawk of a bird, as one alive tissue of being.

From time to time, people needing respite from the deafening arousal of the protest or who simply grew curious came across to join us for a spell. As these elements folded into one another—the money-hungry sales of devastating arms, the spitting and cursing rage and grief of a "peace" protest, the light solace of softly falling rain pattering down on my hat, and our small company of stillness in the midst of fury—it slowly grew hard to find a place in which it wasn't possible to say, "It's my fault," accepting the whole of the moment as the light of that moment.

When you refrain from separating out and judging right and wrong, that quietly radical act of including yourself seamlessly with a situation seems to save all the many beings, including yourself. For we all arrive together with the entire universe, so how can the whole of it not also be our fault, which issues a general amnesty toward all faultfinding? Discernment remains, keener than before, but now becomes a place with a lot more room in it once cleared of blame. Meanwhile, an energy that seems to care for the whole of it—strangely, like love—arises.

With nothing truly separate from you, what can become visible then, as a project, an action, an art form, a practice, a way to move the needle? With the strange blessing of broad acceptance implied in "It's my fault," the whole world (which is medicine) comes along with you.

UNSCATHED IN FIRE

If you can happily wonder, Why should I not sit and be ignited by this shining world? Then can you equally and willingly wonder, Why should I not sit and be ignited by this painfully broken world?

If a lotus were not the form of love that is a radically inclusive state of mind, could it endure such a world as ours unscathed? Or might it actually work the other way around, such that love most fully discovers itself in not shrinking away, but coming to meet this moment of vertiginous change? Hakuin is unequivocal on this point:

> Because the lotus that blooms in the water withers when it comes near fire, fire is the dread enemy of the lotus. Yet the lotus that blooms from the midst of flames becomes all the more beautiful and fragrant the nearer the fire rages. . . . Why should this be so? It is because the fire is the lotus and the lotus is the fire.[3]

We all know the flames of hatred, anger, and grief. We know the flames of despair for life, despair for humanity, and how profoundly our feelings can lay waste to us. How is it that clarity can bloom "all the more beautiful and fragrant" when the inferno of strong feelings is directly met?

How does a mind at home in the fire of the passions proceed? Zhaozhou, once more, gives a pointer that goes beyond all limiting concepts. A monk asks him, "What is meditation?" Fair question, one that every time you sit you ask, and then let it resolve in you.

Zhaozhou replies, "It's not meditation." The monk receives nothing, all better and worse burned away in three words. End of all advice, beginning of all inquiry and unfolding!

"Then what is it?" demands the monk.

"It's alive," says Zhaozhou. "It's alive!" Alive in the very question. Alive in the heart of the one who asks. One alive reality. Nothing can be carved out of it, and meditation can only accede to this (and help us do so).

Alive mind and equally alive reality cannot be separated if we are even half alive to the call of our moment on Earth. "It's alive!" is discovered and recovered over and over again in zazen, and its not-knowing fullness opens our hands and eyes in koans. Hakuin brushed a snail on a leaf to place alongside his trenchant calligraphy that said, "Meditation in the midst of activity is a hundred thousand times better than meditation in stillness." Moving and unmoving, there is nothing outside this complete "alive!"

BENDING

Zhaozhou was asked, "What about when there is a hair's breadth of differentiation?"

He replied, "Course."

"Course" turns a questioner back to the path. There it is— resolving or healing that no-gap is the path itself. This monk's sense of self is still in front of his circumstances, where self-dis-satisfaction and faultfinding can proliferate with ease. Stay with the trouble, bear with uncertainty, give it the full attention of not-knowing, and then is reality *divided*?

Moreover, "Whatever confronts you, don't believe it," Linji quietly mutters in your ear. First and foremost, seize the opportunity to notice what leaps up in your defense, and don't believe it. Turn instead in the vulnerable direction of, What am I afraid of here? Or equally, What are they afraid of here?

This first movement of not-knowing is a chance to stay with reality and with the other, to not turn your back or sour your heart or limit your response, but to bend usefully with the flow of the current. Whenever you feel so very right, you're already becoming wrong. At the heart of this not-knowing is silence, which is a general amnesty extending in all directions, friendlier and more intelligent than the need to be right or even to understand.

But the questioning monk presses further: "What about when the situation is responded to?"

Zhaozhou replies with a potent one-word koan for our times, gathering up not-knowing into the most congruent possible action and offering it here now, under the sign of climate crisis: "Bending."

Bending is undivided. Bending is deep adaptation. Bending does not break reality in two or interrupt the fragile homeostasis of a situation, whether the homeostasis of atmosphere and climate or the emotional climate of engagement with others in bringing about our human rebalancing and tending of the Earth.

Deep adaptation includes resting in the amplitude of no-self, with nothing, or very little, of "me" imposed on the moment. With the sudden arrival of COVID-19, we at first appeared to bend with astonishing speed in the name of public health, before angry fear began to splinter that solidarity. Accelerating climate change across decades has seen governments largely braced against rather than bending in response to the reality of how deeply it threatens health, shelter, and food security, and trashes the dazzling Holocene riches of life on Earth.

Bending in Zhaozhou's sense is like Dogen's subtle and deeply intuitive advice to "turn things while turning with things." The mind of not-knowing can find its way to follow the Dao through difficult circumstances, to soften hard reactions and avoid "coming over all unnecessary." "Bending" then becomes simply what you do that can be of some help in our time of brittle, rackety distress.

When Ciming Chuyuan (986–1039) was asked, "What is the Way?" he replied, "Though stepped on, it does not anger."

With just a little ambiguous wordplay in Chinese with the character for "Way," he is saying that anger can be turned to inform but not possess you, that in the midst of its fire can be found a calmly transforming response far wiser than any reactive impulse. Zhaozhou's "Bending" is exactly such a response. Here's a beautifully telling example:

Robina Courtin, a well-known Australian Tibetan Buddhist nun who is notable for her impatience with undue holiness, was attending an event with her sister in New York City. As they came out onto the street at night, a man stepped forward and threatened her with a knife, demanding that she give him her money. While her sister gasped and began to fumble for her purse, Robina simply said in a firm, reasonable tone, "No. You give me *your* money!"

The completely unexpected nature of her response pulled the rug out from under the man, raising unexpected questions in the path of a violent demand. Her insightful response let the man glimpse himself accurately mirrored but in calm, coherent form, deflecting his attack.

He moved off swiftly, head down, and did not look back. Robina's response was quick enough to eschew reactive fear or anger, and nimble enough to find the aikido kind of move that could safely meet this man's violence without opposing it. Her calm refusal to tolerate the violence he offered undid it for him beautifully, meeting him as a human being, beyond judgment.

Ciming's "it does not anger," though not necessarily easy,

holds out the vital chance to learn how to turn situations around with the transformative power of anger's energy, which comes from a place deeper than right and wrong, a place empty of self and other.

This is lotus in the midst of fire, the endlessly creative path of deep adaptation within crisis.

CODA: ME AND YOU

In late 2022, Abdirashid Abdi, a Somalian refugee living for several decades in Australia who has contributed much to his adopted country, was quietly cycling through empty suburban Brisbane streets in the early hours of the morning when a woman in a large SUV began pursuing him, revving her car loudly behind him and striking him from behind while screaming racist abuse and saying she was going to kill him. Terrified, he swerved off across a vacant block of land, but she crashed through fences to come after him, trying again and again to run him down. Dry-retching in fear, he tried unsuccessfully to raise the alarm in the darkened nearby houses, but finally managed to contact emergency services. Every detail of this horror was duly recorded by the GoPro on his bike helmet.

His victim statement confirmed the impact the attack had on his health, confidence, and ability to work. But then events took an astonishing turn when Abdi expressed only concern and sympathy for the woman. He pleaded for his tormentor to be shown compassion, asking her to seek help and "transform your life."

The judge conceded to his wishes, and his statement reads, "He might be entitled to feel unmitigated enmity toward you. Instead, he has made a most remarkable request for me to show you the compassion that you denied him. He tells me he finds no peace in your incarceration because he believes prison is not the right place for you to receive the help you need. All in all, it's one of the most extraordinary documents I've ever seen produced in these courts."[4] The woman was immediately released on parole, though disqualified from driving for two years.

Abdi said, "I choose to forgive her because I believe that compassion and forgiveness is justice in itself." A lotus blooming in the midst of fire, a fire that conjoins "me" and "you" and cannot set them finally apart—is there anything outside this fire?

A monk comes to Zhaozhou, asking, "What is the sangha?"

Zhaozhou replies, "What else is there but it?"

While the immediate meaning of the word *sangha* is the community of practitioners, through Zen eyes it cannot possibly stop there. The community of an awakened heart-mind radiates out to include all living things, and in a world as dynamic as this Earth, "all living beings" is not restricted only to other creatures but also includes rivers, mountains, stars, forests, trees, blades of grass, fallen sticks—the entire seamless community of life.

And let's do away with even the "it" in "What else is there but it?" Just this silvery-blue morning, a few ragged clouds showing up, here and there dulling the glitter of the early morning dew . . .

The monk presses Zhaozhou further: "Then what is a *person* of the sangha?" How do you live something so vast and all-inclusive?

Looking back at the singular human being facing him, Zhaozhou's down-to-earth reply, like Earth herself, gives it all away: "Me and you."

This not-two in all living beings turns up as "me and you" in every awakened encounter, whether a person, a feeling, a river of ants at work on the kitchen counter, the moist ground under your feet when you walk out after the rains that at last extinguished the megafire. Every moment of being manifests in relationship with the intimacy of some "other" (which is ultimately no other). Being is only interbeing; what else is there but it?

There is no *me*, comma, and *you*. Just *me-and-you*, always arriving together, me-and-you healing into each other. The depth of the *and* in *me-and-you* is the breadth of this universe. The whole Earth, her ecosystems, and the entire cosmos turns on this mutuality. Everything moves together.

Me-and-you comes to life in the willingness to feel, recognize, and understand the pain of another being or a collapsing ecosystem or a living planet catching fire. When anger and fear are recognized as forms of suffering, suffering can turn into the grace of compassionate action. Teaching our own demons to sit requires keeping our heart open even in hell, maintaining companionable mind.

We wake up on Earth, Earth wakes us, wakes up as us, and we wake up as not other than Earth. Me-and-you. Who verifies whom? "I am here so you can be here" is the force of Zhaozhou's me-and-you, which is intent on noticing, softening, and healing, and in offering the *and* in which all beings meet, and this very being meets itself in the other.

This is the best and hardest work of all for we hot-hearted, hot-headed mammals. It wakes us up to be more fully human, present, and here now at a time when we are being continually pushed to consume and exhaust the living world. It waits—it *longs*—to lay bare the grief in our anger and fear so that we can recognize in that grief the two-way flow of suffering *with* the Earth.

It waits and longs to realize a powerful mutual healing, a true reconciliation of all that is so at fault in how we have alienated ourselves from the Earth.

> recent argument
> her spit sizzles
> on the clothes-iron

Part Three

THE WHOLE EARTH
IS MEDICINE

It's the literal body of the Earth, this Buddha.

—DANE CERVINE

火

6

THE FIRE, EARTHED

This Earth has an Aboriginal culture inside.

—DALY PULKARA, YARRALIN ELDER

The blazing fire is expounding the Dharma to all the buddhas of
the three times,
and they are standing on the ground and listening.

—YUNMEN

One time I was walking with my students in the beautiful sandstone Darkinjung country just northwest of Sydney, where the
distinguished Yuin elder Uncle Max Dulumunmun Harrison
had joined us at the end of a seven-day Zen sesshin. A teaching walk with an elder is semisilent, with no destination in mind
apart from the many points where Country (the extraordinarily
rich sense of presence that this chapter shall endeavor to bring to
light) "poked through," beckoning him to stop and draw us in to
its conversation. Close to eighty years old, he leaned from time
to time on the long staff he liked to walk with in later years.

Walks in Country are slow. They proceed at the speed of close, relaxed attention, for the teachings lie latent in every detail, from the barely discernible seepage of water across a track, to that mighty grandmother tree burned down to her core by lightning strike, yet alive in all her edges.

Suddenly Uncle Max said, "Look at that!" pointing to a sign slung between two posts where the rough track crossed the creek and struggled to continue on the other bank. It read, "Private Property Keep Out."

"Where's the private property?" he asked.

We all looked around at the trees, sky, tiny pink orchids peeking their head above the grass, bees softly bothering wattle, clouds drifting, breeze stirring the canopy and lifting the good smell of creek water to our noses, creek music weaving us in, feet cooled with sandy mud . . . then back to the implacably divisive claim on that cold metal sign over which a vine was beginning to make a kindly attempt to rehabilitate it.

That sign breached all that was so present as one abundant offering. "Private Property Keep Out" signals a mind intensely trained on its own small story of a separate self and anxious ownership. Dangling there, alien among the soft green of the trees and scent of wattle, that sign became a koan, startling even itself as it turned all customary assumptions upside down.

Children love looking at things upside down. They know how interesting the world immediately becomes with sky below, earth above, and everything seen brand-new in a startling rearrangement of preconceptions. Try it: face away from what you want to see, bend over with your legs apart, and look through them to glimpse the upside-down view. Everything is sharp, with a charged energy of presence, as though seen for the first time. Freed of the focal point that is yourself, you catch a glimpse of how the Earth sees, with every eloquent detail taking part in one communing. You begin to catch a glimpse of Country.

But the other thing turned upside down that day when Country used that sign to speak was all that comes under the aegis of property law: the entire presence of the Earth translated into mere use value and the creation and defense of wealth, the isolation of a carved-out self, and the overstated claims of talking mind when overheard by a closely listening mind.

Xuefeng says, "All the buddhas of the past, present, and future are turning the great wheel over the blazing fire." The great wheel of the Dharma is turned by every koan over the fire of emptiness that transforms mind.

But Yunmen took Xuefeng's words and turned them upside down to reveal a fresh salience that reaches right through to our times: "Rather, the blazing fire is expounding the Dharma to all the buddhas of the three times, and they are standing on the ground and listening."

"Standing on the ground and listening" is exactly the mood and invitation of Country. Country brings the seamless, ecological dharma of the Earth to inform the Dharma of the buddhas, a critically important, direct transmission that lies beyond scriptures, beyond the talking mind.

This indigenous template of knowledge, won from tens of millennia of deep adaptation to the place that formed it, offers a powerful medicine to our time of crisis. Its specific ecological intelligence is imaginatively whole with all that lives, and it does not imply an impossible return to a preindustrial or preagricultural way of human life. Rather, it implies that the potent dreams and ideas of the Earth can and must be found here now in our own hands, feet, lungs, and intima, in the crucible of our present crisis, and in the most imaginative stretch of our minds within this teetering civilizational moment.

I think the fire of our circumstances demands that we accept this offer. This chapter takes a Zen walk in Country, seeking the medicine that is the whole Earth to help us transform the sickness of our times. If we are to begin to bring the intelligence of emptiness to a collapsing world, find openings for an awakened mind on a planet strewn with crises, and navigate a time in which we are to be torn into greater wholeness if we are to survive, then the living knowledge base that still manifests in First Peoples' deeptime experience of Earth is an essential and formidable gift. Their living knowledge of intimate relationship with Country includes vast past experience of deep adaptation within dramatic climate changes.

It would be madness to refuse its open, outstretched hand.

THE KOAN OF COUNTRY

Country is a richly unfolding koan that unfolds us. It is a matter resolved only in its embodiment. I take it as a koan posed to our fragile time, a time that too much resembles Yanguan's elaborate, profoundly costly, but superfluous and now-broken rhinoceros-horn fan. Country says just bring reality—the obdurate, irreplaceable rhinoceros itself—back whole and alive. This template of mind as mutual companionship with the Earth is a gift from the very earliest human past all the way to now. Country is a touchstone for every heart and mind roused to protect the Earth from the worst impulses in ourselves.

That day when Uncle Max asked, "Where's the private property?" the words of Auntie Beryl Carmichael, "If you're not in connectedness, you're not in reality," leapt to mind. A mind softened and prepared by days of Zen meditation falls more readily open to the wisdom so generously shared by these indigenous elders, for the practice of Zen koan's not-knowing follows Country's etiquette of "come in from the side, sit awhile, and wait to be invited in."[1]

It may be the earthy Daoist roots of Zen that make it so receptive to the protocols of being in Country. The receptive not-knowing mind that zazen grows can subdue the push of thought so as to notice and attend to just what is appearing to the senses, so as to begin to inhabit the space between thoughts, free of opinions that would replace what's happening. Likewise, the mind awake in Country subdues itself to closely listen to, hear, sing, and be permeated by what Country feels, wants, knows. The one prepares the way for the other.

Paying close attention to what is happening just where you are and just as you are reclaims your inseparability from the physical world, and reconsecrates its essential mystery and presence. This kind of attention lets Country begin to think along with you. Substitute for a moment the whole Earth for Country, and the offer that lies here for our climate-stressed times begins to reveal itself.

Country offers deeply human forms of Aboriginal Dreaming in stories, songlines,[2] ceremonies, and physical place. These are epic stories of living knowledge, revealed and lived practically and requiring a yielding absorption of mind into place. Somewhat similarly, each Zen koan is a living fragment of an epic— one mind, one masterpiece that is ultimately inseparable from this Earth. And it sings us up more alive and together with the place where we are.

In both traditions, story is a vital instrument of transmitting the teachings and testing how deeply you see. Dreaming stories are songlines that make the world, containing multiple levels of entry depending on initiation. The koan path also offers a way of stories that make little literal sense to the conventional mind, but open in a vastly different light when seen from the ground of emptiness. And koans, like songlines, are the living footprints of the ancestors. They do not create the physical world as the Dreaming does, but like the Dreaming, they bring us to where we can see more clearly the place where we are and how it calls to us.

Perhaps the affinity between the two can be characterized this way: Country is profound Earth dharma inhabiting the hearts and forming the minds of those alive to it; Zen is buddhadharma completely earthed and waking up this human form. What we might do with such a template for deeper congruence with the Earth, well, that's in our hands.

INSIDE MIND

Daly Pulkara, the late Yarralin "lawman"—meaning someone initiated into a high degree of responsibility for Country—from the Victoria River region of northwest Australia, once commented, "This Earth has an Aboriginal culture inside."

Uncle Daly's words are not just asking us to listen for something hidden in the body of Australian indigenous lore. They're not even a claim for the overarching importance and original force of indigenous wisdom. He's making a simple point, one that he found obvious: the awakened human mind is latent in the Earth. The awakened human mind is discovered in and informed by the nature of the Earth, found to be complete with the Earth, and expressed in the actions of care for Country—the practical, intimate attentiveness and ecological competence that marks maturity as a human being. This "us-two" of human and Earth is natural and arrives always joined. Each completes the other so that an Aboriginal culture can be said to be discovered intimately *inside* the Earth, as the Earth is inside it.

In Country, as in Zen practice, there is a willingness to be *un*-made, at least to a degree, and a willingness to become more reliably fit to meet the task of congruence with a planet in perilous crisis. The willing sacrifice of a watertight self is the healing back into . . . *what?* Something rightly difficult to name. Best not to litter it with attempts. It has no surface for names. "Country" is just about right.

WALKING IN COUNTRY

"The miracle is to walk on the Earth."

When Linji said this, he didn't bother adding, "awake," as in "to walk awake on the Earth," since whether awake or not, we walk on a miracle. My Zen path has always been psychologically barefoot, sometimes literally so. I rarely wore shoes until I was eight, and as for Zen Dharma, its roots in me have sought deeper intimacy with the Earth from the beginning. The wonder of the Earth drew me into the richness of not-knowing that informs every step of Zen and leads only deeper into that wonder.

Sensing the affinity and shared ground between the Dharma apparently coming from an Asian "elsewhere" and the Dreaming anciently revealed in this continent raises a vital question: Can I belong to this without transgressing? As an inheritor of unearned settler advantage, someone who can presume no simple right of entry to Aboriginal culture, I find the answer in the question itself. It comes back as, "Yes. Always ask." Follow the protocols, beginning with, "Only don't 'know.'"

Country is reciprocity itself. What it wants us to know opens only to a respectful, unpresuming, attentive, not-knowing mind.

Over the last twenty-five years, until Uncle Max's death in March 2022, I walked at length in Country dozens of times with him. Our decades of friendship critically shaped my sense of how to earth the fire of Zen Dharma right here in the exacting and unrepeatable place where I am. I deeply mourn his passing.

Uncle Max grew up in the fringe community of Wallaga Lake, at the foot of the sacred south coast mountain known in Yuin language as Gulaga, though named Mount Dromedary by Captain Cook for its distinctive twin peaks. The formal schooling he was offered as an Aboriginal child was pointedly scanty, yet his education was immense. Because his mother held a lot of important Law (as in the Aboriginal sense of initiated knowledge and responsibility for Country), he was fully initiated into indigenous Law and would share lore he had received from the five remarkable elders he often called "those old scientists." He carried no blame or anger for the injustices of his life, holding instead to the integrity of taking your own inventory and not leaning too far into someone else's. "It comes down only on us," he said—an enduring and excellent koan for our times.

Across the decades of our walks in Country and the public talks and other events we conducted together, I was privileged to bring Zen understanding into contact with indigenous lore in many and varied public contexts—religious, educational, and cultural. Each time offering just a simple us-two in easy sync, I'd seat Zen mind respectfully and companionably alongside the indigenous mind he brought alive through his vivid stories, their subtle intent reaching deep by making generous room for laughter. As Tyson Yunkaporta notes, "If you're not laughing, you're not learning."[3] By trusting the latent concordance between these two traditions, the earthed current in my Zen Dharma quietly deepened, and the Aboriginal culture within Zen quietly discovered itself in me.

It had no choice. As Dogen says, "When you know the place where you are, practice begins." Zen Dharma sits on the Earth and stands up here, in me, in red earth and saltbush, shadows of wallabies, brilliant skies, fire, and rain. It has no choice, for this is the way awakening moves. In Australia, Zen can't help but find its feet on the songline of the Way.

US-TWO

"Us-two" is the great indigenous Australian undoing of the way most languages insistently lean on strict subject-object definitions and differences in order to construct meaning. Can language be induced beyond its subject-object dependency into the realm of *no*-subject, *no*-object? Or to put it another way, into one net of communing? Tyson Yunkaporta brings into English the dual first-person pronoun *us-two*, which derives from indigenous Aboriginal languages to describe a live encounter that constantly resolves two subjectivities. In the case of Country, us-two is the human being and the sentient place where you are proceeding together, continually bringing each other to life.

"Us-two" companionably joins Zhaozhou's "me-and-you" in recognizing a world of interbeing that does not separate "me" and "you." In the "and" of "me-and-you," care for Country arises together with and the imperative to collectively protect and heal the Earth. This is a healing that can move only through a flowing exchange in mutual relationships. In every encounter between the self and the other, whether that other is human, nonhuman, or more than human, it is the sacred play of exchange between subjectivities that realizes the place where we are.

The miracle of your walking on the Earth: your feet *and* the Earth, me-*and*-you, us-two. One touch.

When challenged as to what could possibly approve—even require—his profound commitment to awakening as he sat there, immovable, under the bodhi tree, the Buddha simply reached down and touched the earth. That enlightened, confirming touch—it's mutual. It has no choice. So it is with Country, which is the human-Earth compact that both generates and awakens in our hearts and minds the deep imprint of the relationships that hold things together.

In indigenous Australia, how were these great matters traditionally taught? With a human finger tenderly touching the earth, tracing the pattern charged with that knowledge in receptive sand. Such knowledge respectfully seeks not to dispel the mystery of earth, fire, wind, water, mountain, and waves but to move in accord with it. Knowledge comes to us and becomes clear to us only when we come to it empty-handed.

DRAWN IN SAND

The us-two sand pattern is quite elementary: a dot, a line, then another dot. That is us-two in its infinite possible variety.

But here's the thing: the line between those two points in the sand, *that* is the whole matter, subtending the two dots, the two points of sentience. Following Zhaozhou, let's call those two points of intimacy "me-and-you." That connective charge offered by "and" is what actualizes and completes each of those points and is the living dynamic of discovery, inquiry, and learning. It is the interbeing that is interanimating all our lives, with each other and with supposedly inanimate things. Has water, for example, ever refused your touch or declined entry to your body leaping into it? This incoming breath in your nose and chest right now—did it hesitate to come in and fully meet you? In every contact, you share one beginningless communion event.

The relational line of mutuality in the dot-stroke-dot creation pattern is always here when you notice that it is. Both Zen and indigenous wisdom are founded on the idea of getting past ourselves enough to begin *noticing*, and standing on the ground and listening.

That simple pattern can freely join from one of its dots via a fresh line in the sand to another dot, which then joins to another dot, to another, and another, and another . . . Eventually you begin to notice you have the infinitely branching and intricate net of Indra, but now presented as the vast, evolving interconnectedness of us-two's, as one ecosystem of sentience.

The indigenous version of the net of Indra is highly particular in its interests—not this jewel, that jewel, but instead wombat, dingo, rockface, sandbank, waterhole, swooping goshawk—at once recognizing and interconnecting the sentient presence of each vividly present living thing. Country is never anything in general. Instead, in Country, each being is dignified as an embodiment of the whole. Country's caretaking call to us lies precisely here.

Koans makes that kind of caretaking awareness intimate. You can recognize the entire universe in that rockface, those drops falling in ice melt, the fray in this feather, the curl of that toenail clipping, the thud of this heartbeat. Then the wholeness of this finds it hard not to flower into custodial caring toward of all your kin. It's a loving awareness, hard to separate from the place where you are. And why would you even try?

The caring intrinsic to Country is as natural in the end as what flows from the not-knowing of Zen: "This too is me. This is my body. This is my most personal face." Call it a kind of ongoing regenerative adaptation to reality coming alive as awakened mind in Zen, and coming pointedly awake as active caring for the life of Country.

Country stores what truly matters safely earthed in deep time and place, and lodged in the mind and imagination in the Dreaming stories. It can be degraded but not lost, wounded but never stripped of its regenerative power. When mind is *located*, us-two flourishes in ten thousand forms in all four directions, and listening and seeing begins.

For starters, it is visible in land that is held in mind and cared for with respect and gratitude for human and more-than-human life.

QUIET COUNTRY

Daly Pulkara stared out at a desecrated landscape of spectacular soil erosion in the Victoria River area of the Kimberley region of northwestern Australia. The erosion was caused by widespread tree-clearing, along with overgrazing cattle that had trampled waterholes and destroyed riverbanks. Gazing at it alongside him, anthropologist Deborah Bird Rose asked, "What do you call this?" Daly replied, "It's the wild. Just the wild." The life of that country was visibly falling down in those gullies and washing away with the rains. And his words washed away any romantic (yet subtly self-hating) notion of "the wild" as a wilderness mercifully free of human presence, weirdly bereft of human minding.

Pressed, he went on to speak of "quiet country," country in which all the care of generations of people is evident and present to those who know how to see it. Held in mind and heart, sung and tended in ceremony and in directly practical forms of care, the resilient ease of "quiet country" stands in stark contrast with the ignorance and gross neglect that would allow a vast landscape of outstanding ecological integrity to degrade into an unloved "wild, just the wild." He was, of course, describing what is at stake in Country.

The real, trackless wilderness is inside those who let it fall from its natural state of grace. Meanwhile, Country is always in conversation with us. Nothing can mute its voice except us.

AN EARTHED SPIRITUALITY

The Buddha walked the Earth in the Axial Age, a time when literacy was flowering in different civilizations. Yet the ground of his luminous awakening was a roaring silence, earlier than words, which flowed through him while he sat on the earth, sheltered by a spreading fig tree. The earliest intimation of that silence is said to have touched him as a small boy half-drowsing under a rose apple tree, when he fell gently into a vast openness of radiant well-being, a happiness of such simple directness that adult life left him warily suspicious of it.

Why do I fear this happiness? He wondered as he remembered the touch of that direct breath of reality in his childhood. He resolved to abandon his former austerities and distancing doubts and to sit there, entire with the earth, the tree, the breeze, the morning star.

Wherever Buddhism has traveled it has encountered older existing forms of spirituality such as Tibetan Bön, Chinese Daoism, and Japanese Shinto—and despite the millions of words that gradually accreted to it, an affinity with a fully earthed form of spiritual orality and basis of mind came as naturally as groundwater to these new expressions of the Dharma. In fact, translator David Hinton sees Chan (Zen) to be a rich spiritual ecology, shaken alive by Buddhism, as an extension of Daoism.[4] Daoism has the capacity for breathing human and Earth in one breath; the relaxed, slanted gaze of its teaching stories don't bother to sort out the human from the more-than-human realm. They show no trace of regarding the natural world, or the mortality that enlivens it, with suspicion. They understand that nothing is held back in the natural world, neither life nor death, and by this unparalleled generosity we test our human limits for gratitude and forbearance.

Hinton examines the Chinese character that English renders as "understanding" and finds "a capacity that human thought and emotion share with wild landscape and, indeed, the entire Cosmos."[5] The character reflects an ancient Chinese assumption that humans and nonhumans form a single sentient tissue that thinks and wants—thought held not as something separate and looking out onto reality from inside a human skull, but wholly woven into the generative flow of a living, intelligent cosmos.

Country confides its own intricate Dreaming with human minds. The Dreaming of a place then is sung, which means brought to mind, tended in ceremony, and taken up in active care for Country in order to maintain the correct order of relationships that keeps things whole and healed. This masterpiece of human ingenuity has managed to reconcile human civilization through sixty thousand years of dramatic ecosystem changes; its form of deep adaptation possesses and offers to the world a deeply sane, stress-tested, self-correcting Earth intelligence. It is profound tutelage in the work of deep adaptation. And luckily, no amount of obliteration and mindless forgetting can take its song out of the land.

ZEN AND COUNTRY MUTUALLY CONFIDE

Country is entrusted to and embedded in place as its source; place is its direct revelation and expression, its Law library, its vivid Dreaming stories, and the timeless repository for its own safekeeping, ensuring that this long healing of human and Earth into each other cannot vanish or ever be forgotten. The rocks themselves flow with it; they remember and memorialize the story that human ears picked up by deep listening across vast spans of time. Rocks and trees and waters become indented with the words and songs and stories—possibly even the thoughts—of all of we two-legged ones. What a lovely charge of alertness and care comes back to us from this!

Compare this to the rich series of meanings lurking in the word *dharma*: the law, the teachings, *and* each thing and every living being here in its own right, standing up alive and yet utterly interwoven. Mind itself, awake. All of them are discovered in one another, such that Dogen would say, "I came to know that mind is no other than the mountains and rivers and the great wide Earth, the sun, the moon, and the stars."

When you sit on the earth in zazen, you sit in ancient time, elbow-to-elbow with no time at all, an ancestral presence. Here rests the mind and reality of that eternal "well that has never been dug," as Ikkyu put it. Here is its timeless water that "ripples from a stream that does not flow" and from which draws Ikkyu's "someone, with no shadow or form."

It's very difficult to convey the inside of the timeless, non-linear clarity of zazen. You find yourself less an isolated self and more participant in a field of subjectivity with many communing points of aliveness, or like the mycorrhizal net of brilliantly conversant filaments linking trees, or perhaps like a brain streaming and sparking electrical connections that you could never possibly foreshadow, plan, or dream up. Or indeed, like a dream in which all the parts in one continuous realm of emergence are lucid informants of one realization, not available to discursive thought.

More awake still you can find nothing that is not one borderless consciousness and feel not the slightest inclination to move an inch. The music of mortality freely enters this timeless mind and does not contradict it at all. And the song of all things at this level of awareness, what is it?

As Zhaozhou so simply said, "It's alive!"

THE PLACE WHERE YOU ARE

The extraordinary David Banggal Mowaljarlai (1925–1997), painter, teacher, storyteller, and linguist, was a senior Law-holder of the Ngarinyin people in West Kimberley. He called the joy of the awake, skin-to-skin recognition of Country *yorro yorro*, translating this as "everything standing up alive, brand-new."

Yorro yorro opens to you when your vision has opened such that you can see clearly. Dogen's way of expressing this is to say that when the ten thousand things advance and confirm the true nature of this self, that is enlightenment, a matter of joyously humble reverence. And his words, "When you know the place where you are, practice begins" chime with those of Martu elder and University of Queensland professor Mary Graham when she brings the painfully human-centric declaration of Descartes, "I think, therefore I am," back down to earth and gives us, "I am located, therefore I am."

Listen to Mowaljarlai's pure joy in becoming complete with Country, utterly *located*:

> Morning gives you the flow of a new day—aah! . . . You
> go out now, see animals moving, see trees, a river . . .
> Your vision has opened and you start learning now . . .
> Your presence and their presence meet together and you
> recognize each other. These things recognize you. They
> give their wisdom and their understanding to you when
> you come close to them.

"Come close to them" is only possible in the intimacy of not-knowing. He immediately continues: "You got Country as far as the eye can see, and it's yours. But because of this consciousness, you are going through it reverently, quietly."[6] This yielding of self to "the place where you are" is beautiful—no monologue trapped inside a skull, but one fluent conversation, me-and-you, based on respect on both sides: I'm all yours, it says, though for the sharing not the taking. This is Country enjoying itself in the depth of our conversation with its provenance.

Realization likewise lets each thing stand up again alive, brand-new in its timeless and immediate presence. Indeed, you recognize things, animals, trees, a river as they recognize you; your presence and theirs meet so exactly there is no difference at all. Yorro yorro is a state of human ripeness. When you become like this, Mowaljarlai assures us, "then every day one more day is added to your life, you will be one day richer."[7]

COMING FROM THE SIDE

Conversation with Country requires approaching from the side, holding no expectations, and just waiting patiently to be welcomed in. This courtesy is known as "respect law," and only when this essential threshold is well-held will Country consider coming to meet you. Even then, just as with struggling to sit deeply in zazen, we value any difficulty or hesitation for the almost ritual way it initiates you perforce into deeper powers of attention.

Country responds to and depends on our closely listening, which means not supposing a single thing but following, moving with, and acceding to conditions. It means finding the live point of responding, loosening, and letting go of the one-track mind and discovering mind to be the intimate and yet edgeless field of attention. This is the vital shift from the narrow pursuits of linear mind—that hand held sideways, all five fingers pointing in one direction—to the open, radiating, splayed hand of non-linear mind.

There are no straight, predetermining lines in natural forms. The Dao moves as it wishes, like the timeless will of a waterway. Teaching patterns traced into the sand describe how we are with what we are—curved lines and shapes that trace a pattern called "universe," or Earth, or river, or ecocommunity, or rock strata, or kinship, or bloodstream. Like koans, those tracings open a path of awareness that proceeds by means of *not* presuming, *not* presupposing, *not*-knowing. And like koans, they restore us to a more seamless state of being in the most intimate way. Like the intima, the epithelial cells that inform the sense of touch that are the innermost lining of the veins and arteries that carry our lifeblood, this knowing knows us earlier than we know ourselves.

INTERWOVEN BY WHAT YOU LOVE

The season in hell suffered on the east coast of Australia in 2019 and 2020 woke up not only serious fear but also the true depth of how precious is this home place. Under low-hanging fire clouds, we discovered the full radiance of its every beloved detail, together with the whole of its human and more-than-human community. The peril of our times is exactly what stirs us to undertake the long pilgrimage to return the recognizing gaze of the Earth. It is what moves us to restore our intrinsic love for her, come at last to finally pay our respects, offer our listening, and let Country rearrange us back to right where we are.

As Mary Graham says, "We become human in the places most precious to us." The land that grows us up and makes us human teaches us love. Country, wherever you are on Earth, is the place where you are when its preciousness comes alive in you together with other people and all creaturely life. There's a deeply affectionate, family feeling here—it is love that lets the Earth confide its own stories to us; it is love that attunes us to what sings and speaks in the land and how it offers direction.

This is a love that concedes the overall advantage not to personal advantage ("Private Property Keep Out") but to the Earth. "You belong," says Country in its embrace. The Earth has never stopped saying an entirely mutual, "I'm all yours." To clearly hear the profound generosity in this, to find it inscribed on your skin and engraved on your bones, obviates human rapaciousness.

Graham explains how a mere survival ethos is essentially isolating to anyone who holds it. Survival mind assumes there to be a contesting "them" and "us," or an "it" and "me," which unwittingly ensures a hostile environment. A relational ethos, by contrast, is sensitive, empathic, and has the valuable, practical capacity to self-correct early on. It is the continual nudge of the understanding that we must be interwoven to come into balance.

In Country's terms, the deep adaptation we seek is the practice of continually interweaving ourselves back into balance by keeping the Earth "sung," meaning held in the imagination, heart, and psyche, and tended in the ceremonially aware mind, with its self-aware routines of taking care of what is. And in so doing, we safely move from a parasitical to an informed caretaking relationship with the Earth, one that sings us up as necessary, valuable, even essential.

Country is understood to be the oldest living Elder of any indigenous clan or group. The entire business of care for Country naturally follows from that understanding, and rather than avoiding difficulty or discomfort, care for Country finds the deep *savor* of relationship right there.

Us-two, over and over again. It's not a passive business.

MUTUALLY SAVE, MUTUALLY SAVE

Xutang Zhiyu (1185–1269), in his *Record of Empty Hall*, brings this matter forward in the following case:

Xitang Zhizang asks his assembly of monks, "Strive, but for what?"

A monk comes forward and places both hands palm-down on the ground, right where he sits.

Xitang asks, "What are you doing?"

"We save each other!" the monk replies.

He's right, but Xitang presses him further: "A teacher for this great assembly, yet there is more."

Xitang's words contain an invitation into humility; however, this monk shakes out his sleeves in a traditional gesture implying "nothing can be added to nothing," and leaves the hall.

Where's the activity of *saving* and where's the *mutual* in that monk? Not risking getting those two hands dirty, it seems, just staying "safely" with the idea of saving. Purity can be a prison within clarity. So, what is this "more"?

According to Tyson Yunkaporta, the word for "safety" is pointedly absent from the more than five hundred Aboriginal languages once spoken across the Australian continent. Yet each language has multiple words suggesting the natural human obligations of "protection" and "protecting." "Safety" summons a survivalist mindset, which ushers unsafety into mind, while "protection" subtends a relational one, which shelters everything.

I hear the mind of "care for Country" alive and well in Xitang's request to see that there is more. Unlived, this monk's "We save each other"—also translatable as "Mutually save, mutually save!"—remains inert, trapped short of application in the world. But the wisdom of Country, vested in the Dreaming, is both active and utilitarian. It is a living knowledge realized in the act of being applied in order to improve and care for present and future circumstances. It is drawn from a deep-time well of memory of being born and living sustainably on a land base and the sense of being integral to that land base. In turn, this sense of belonging is psychically transformed into the potent mnemonics of storytelling, art, and ceremony, recommitting this living oral knowledge back to the safekeeping of place.

This is the actively caretaking mind that breathes air and has traction. It lives locally but is evolving. Like any open, living system, it is alive to sudden eruptions of change. It is high-value use-knowledge, bred into the bones by living as an essential participant in that land base and remaining attuned to the subtle inner sentience of Country that generates the field of visible and tangible "outside" ecological relationships. The even more subtle "inside" pattern of Country instructs a human being how to become more congruent, to evolve and move with its discernible patterns of emergence, in a way that is culturally attuned to a more-than-human world.

If we stray too far outside this informing set of patterns of creation, we deny the terms of the Earth and universe, and the fact that all life, not just human life, participates in creating the ecology of the Earth.

These patterns speak and sing from Earth's point of view. Whether traced in sand, painted on bodies, trees, or the walls of caves, or found in stories encoded in the Dreamings, all of them say, "Mutually save, mutually save." They are the patterns that take on character and think and speak with the eloquence and sustaining coherence of any creature or complex ecosystem. There is a sacred play of exchange between them. They sing up the timeless source of endless changes. This is to concede at every point that the Earth has her own astonishing Dreaming, and our long-neglected human job is to attune to her subtle signal, beyond the noise and interruption of our busy, self-important minds.

You can understand the "inside" current of ancient Dreaming stories as the tendency of the Earth to heal the gap forced by human minds. Truly notice the inner patterns being manifest in the land, and the Earth flows in you. The poetry of the Earth, pressing through to form human wisdom and story, is living knowledge.

MIND OF FOREST

Rich ecological complexities that appear stable over time behave as though a form of intelligence is guiding them, responsible for them, protecting them.

One time, traveling and walking with Uncle Max in Country, he suddenly directed us down a side road to check out what was happening up on a sandstone shelf formation. It was at a point where wildfire had raced uphill through the tree canopy below and licked just over its edge, scorching this mossy green "hanging swamp" that normally was fully charged with water and dripping into the trees below, and in heavy rain becomes a waterfall that feeds a perennial creek.

We found the moss to be barely moist, crumbly to the touch, and the scorched bushes and shrubs growing close to the edge of the ledge, still fire-withered and fragile. Yet astonishingly, just a little farther up the slope where the trees were untouched by fire, the ground was squelchy-wet underfoot. How could it possibly be that the water was failing to follow gravity down the slope of the rock shelf and make the scorched area wet? Uncle Max just said, "Well, when somebody's badly burned, you don't give them big gulps of water, do you? You just give little sips at a time. These fellas up here, they're just holding the water back at the right rate, taking care of those little fellas down there."

Grateful and astonished, we were eased into sharing the presence and mind of the forest, which is the inside of care for Country. It's the sense of being lifted into the more-than-human community seen in the act of observing and caring for each point of sentience.

UNHURRIED ANCESTOR TIME

The deepest theme of the Earth is its embodied time.

Both Zen practice and Country open to no-time, thereby consummating the present in the very act of exhausting its apparent limits. We're in touch with the time enjoyed by all things in the empty aeon, the eye opening to that seamless reality. Like the Zen ancestors, the indigenous ancestor beings of the Dreaming and the old ones of the recent past are all right here now—not so much behind us in a linear kind of time past, but walking ahead, drawing us deeper in through the gate of unknowing. When we recognize and become intimate with the mind of an ancestor in koan practice, we walk and talk with them and see eye-to-eye while sharing the same eye.

To experience time unopposed to life and to awakening changes the nature of time, as does all intense and sustained spiritual practice. When we see this way, the striking temporal fluidity of the Dreaming opens to us as a simple and evident "everywhen," to use the term coined by the esteemed twentieth-century anthropologist W. E. H. Stanner. What time has ever been fixed in a dream? Mind awakens into the great dream of the Earth, alive fact of reality. Meanwhile, the pathos of the moment we're in unfolds in accelerating linear time, with delineated beginnings and endings. Without agreed-on measurements of time to synchronize business, how could the relentless acceleration of unending "progress," wealth creation, and technology dedicated to strip-mining every inch of time even be conceived, let alone coordinated?

Country helps strike the imaginal flint we need to light a cool, healing fire on this Earth—a fire to temper fire. Then the immediate, anxious thought: is there enough time?

Country *is* time. And so time is fruitfully dark and deep-lying in Country. It is nonlinear, affirming through unending changes its unchanging source. This no-time awareness opens to the possibility of our continually learning from—or better, within—deep time, and designing for a time deeper and richer than what is measured by the bottom line. This nonlinear time suggests a storehouse of regenerative knowledge, always there to restore, repurpose, retrofit, and deeply adapt within change.

In the 2006 Australian film *Ten Canoes*, we hear the late, beloved indigenous actor and dancer David Gulpilil speaking in voiceover, teasingly unmooring us from ticktock time and drawing us into everywhen. The camera tracks slowly past a stretch of nondescript shrubs, bushes, grasses, rocks, and trees up in the escarpment country of East Arnhem Land. "Now we're going back," he says as we steadily take in the lapidary quality of every detail as it grows increasingly compelling to our eyes. "Now we've gone a hundred years back, a thousand years back . . . maybe thousand, thousand years back now . . . [chuckles]." And still the bushland, in its utterly contingent, infinitely varied thusness, steadily holds forth the light of no-time.

There is a deeply consoling sense here, an assurance of infinite belonging, just as we are, mortal and all. Such belonging underlies the plain fact that the actions we must take to defend the Earth from ourselves are limited in reach and time, and grief over our apparent failures must be included too, as a necessary part of the ever-evolving whole. That they lie, in the end, beyond final judgment, for nothing is or can be "final."

LITHIC TIME IS ALSO OUR TIME

Up on a saddle just below the peak of Gulaga, that southeast coastal Australian mountain sacred to the Yuin, is a sacred creation and teaching site that has great presence and leaves a deep impression on all who walk through it.

Gulaga features numerous dramatic granite rock formations, each a station for long contemplation. One such formation is a towering three-part pillar of granite that rises to a disappearing point high in the sky. This manifestation of Yuin teaching about time takes the huge base boulder as the infinitely interwoven mystery of your emergence—beginningless, and beyond disentangling. It broadly supports the next long, upright passage of stone, signaling where you are now. I receive it as the contingent or karmic realm of this very life we're in, awake yet half-asleep, doing our best to reconcile life and death while holding as steady as possible.

Of the third stage of the rock formation that pushes upward to reach the sky's vanishing point, little can be said, for it has no measurable time in it at all.

"But the one in the middle is the one that is important for us . . . shows us we're between love and hate, that we're between hot and cold, hunger and fullness, between evil and greatness," says Uncle Max. This infinitely in-between boulder resounds with your own heartbeat. It is the place where we are each called to embody the not-two quality of each breath and the *not*-three nature of time's inner pattern. It holds the continual emergence

of forms to be inseparable equally from deep time, impermanence, and no-time at all.

Gradually you begin to see that all three stones *at once* manifest
our moments under the open sky. This teaching does not present a directional flow of past-present-future so much as all three
forms of presence flowing through one another to manifest this
very moment. If we fully inhabit the place between, the current
of this mysterious life flows like blood through all three. All of
time is within reach in Country. We can rely on ourselves in that
light.

The base rock holds the infinity before your brightly lit time
here, and the summit rock points to the infinity of time after
you "go back in." But the place in-between heals both into each
other, waking up every choice you make in the face of personal
mortality and the enduring life of the Earth. And so this sacred
three-rock teaching is not bound to the ticktock time of *telos*
and an ultimate end, but draws us into where being pervades
the whole universe, existing right here, right now, where every
breath is drawn.

All three rocks comprise us at once. But here in the middle of
the middle, we live with the fact that our every thought, dream,
word, and action is alive with real consequences. This evocation
of lithic time gives us back the wholeness of our true, earthed relationship, in this exquisitely consequential tipping-point moment in
the history of human action exerted upon the earth, this buddha.

SENTIENT EARTH

Zhaozhou's student asks him, "What is Buddha, and what is all
living things?"

"All living things are buddha. Buddha is all living things," replies Zhaozhou.

Is he saying the same thing twice? Surely not.

Buddha means "awake." All living things are this one awake mind, share this empty and complete nature. Thus, "All living things are Buddha" and so cannot help but lend themselves to confirming your own awake mind.

But also, "Buddha is all living things." To wake up is to find all living things looking back at you, curious to see how you will manifest this awakening mind. All care for the Earth arises in this verdant place, and the Earth's verdancy rises with it, alive.

The Yolngu, strong holders of living indigenous knowledge in northeastern Arnhem Land and along the coastline of the Arafura Sea between Australia and western New Guinea, recognize three categories of living things: the first, all things that move or have an effect on other things (the sun, moon, stars, rocks, rivers, wind, glaciers, fire, and so on); the second, all things that breathe or have the ability to reproduce (all plants and creatures on land and in the sea, but interestingly, not human beings).

A third category of living things is reserved just for ourselves, not to elevate our status, but to moderate and discipline our manipulative and destructive tendencies, obliging us to be conscious of our kinship with all other living things. This category of living things needs Law/lore and its obligations and sanctions, and as a crucial rider to all Law, forgiveness. I bow to the wisdom of forgiveness as the secret sustaining power of all kinship and community, and to self-restraint and self-relinquishment as the true gift and basis of custodianship.

Let trees look back at you. Hear the creek sing your complete meaning. Accede to the charge this mind lays on us, its exquisite mutuality. Country enjoys itself fully in our human depth of communion with its provenance, when we get past a self-important, self-referential, self-enclosing self.

We never left the naturally generous embrace of the Earth, though we've rudely slammed a door on it in our minds and apparently fitted that door with case-hardened locks and foolproof codes. Locked-in creatures, staring out at the fullness of reality, are we. But luckily, the genius of koan, as with Country, is mind shaped to pick each lock it has created just as soon as we recognize the necessary and sufficient longing to get free.

THE BELONGING IN THE LONGING

"Mountains belong to those who love them," says Dogen.

Notice the *longing* in the word *belonging*, and the love implicit in the longing. Practice is a kind of yearning to come home and be at rest in the quiet country that is zazen. And we find deep satisfaction in Country too, by holding this very place precious and caring for it accordingly.

True belonging is won by the respect in which love rests. Just put in the loving work, suggests Country. Whether we call it care for Country or practice, it's not much more than exerting ourselves as needed to heal ourselves back more fully into a relaxed and useful presence on the Earth.

The seventeenth-century Chinese Zen master and nun Ziyong Chengru brilliantly evokes the dharma of Country and its natural state of mutual reliance:

> The Dharma does not rise up alone—it can't emerge without your reliance on the world. If I take up the challenge of speaking, I must surely borrow the light and the dark, the form and the emptiness of the mountains and hills and the great Earth, the call of the magpies and the cries of the crows. The water flows and the flowers bloom, brilliantly preaching without ceasing. In this way, there is no restraint.

And in this way, Country realizes itself in us.

Chengru's "no restraint" is a kind of paying of homage that can emerge naturally with practice. After three or four days of silent re-treat, people move at the speed of close attention. They find them-selves bending over to study tiny spiderwebs picked out by dew in the grass, stopping to receive as if in their own bodies the intricate musings of a warbling magpie, dissolving with the fluctuating pattens of leaf shadows on the path. And they find themselves offering an unselfconscious bow of gratitude. All entirely natural. As Zhaozhou says, turning around all stiff resistance to self-relinquishment, "If there was no paying homage, how could it possibly be natural?"

And then, how suddenly unnatural it so obviously is to turn your back on the gift and miss the living offer of the Earth to be complete with us, enjoying our awake consciousness.

STANDING ON THE GROUND AND LISTENING

One time Yunmen asked a student who wandered up to him, "What have you been up to?"

Instead of becoming tongue-tied as was almost customary in Yunmen's formidable presence, this student bravely offers, "I was talking to a rock."

Yunmen asks, "Did the rock respond?"

The student could not respond, so Yunmen answers for him: "That rock was nodding to you long before you spoke."

Country teaches human custodial care—first, of our own im-pulses, and then by pointing out that how we walk on the Earth can exert such crushing, dominating, self-important sway that it misses the incomprehensible privilege of being here. To be a cus-todian of the Earth is to realign with the patterns of creation in a place, becoming alive to its conversation with you.

There's nothing going on in reality but a mutual responding and communing, subject-to-subject, me-and-you. The rocks have been nodding courteously to us long before we drowned their el-oquence in talk. Ever since they proffered the elements of star cataclysms to pour forth into earliest life, their speech poured forth in silence has been forming us. When did we stop noticing, listening, responding, and moving with this ongoing creation event?

Our inability to quiet the talking mind mutes the Earth. Yet with the mind of Zen and Country too, that stone recognizes your true face in the ancient mirror of this Earth, even if you cannot yet recognize and return the courtesy of its graceful nod of recognition. How unflappably it points the way.

THREE OCHRE DOTS, PLUS ONE

The natural etiquette of proceeding in Country as well as observing the formalities that create the transformative ritual space of Zen practice all fell into place for me the day a wise Maori friend told me about how to wear a carved *pounamu*, the sacred greenstone of Aotearoa, the Maori name for New Zealand.

You don't wear your pounamu to the pub or argue or use bad language in its presence, he told me. Instead, when wearing the sacred pounamu, you hold yourself toward it. This is to say you let your awareness of its presence open the way to a more receptive and intelligent awareness of the mind and sensing of the body. Such an unconditioned mind rests in an alert and willing silence with a human heartbeat. Then the mystery to be touched and known with empty hands can wake in you.

Hold yourself like this toward Country; hold yourself like this toward awakening. And hold yourself like this toward the challenge of protecting the Earth from ourselves. This is a ritual form of awareness. The matter here is subtle: not-knowing does not strain to clear up or explain so much as to create a way of holding yourself toward the mysterious with a quiet mind and an alert body, until it is ready to let you in. It will happen the way spring, in its own time, greens the winter-bitten grass.

In the ceremony of proceeding to a sacred site, Uncle Max

would tie on an ochre-red headband and silently apply dots of white ochre to the forehead of each person who will be clapped into the site in order to alert the old ones there to our presence.

First, one dot above each eye—one for alert listening and making sense, and one for moving and acting in accord with listening. Next, a third dot, placed between the other two, acknowledging the third eye, the eye that sees emptiness. No gap, seamless, complete. Right and left, inside and outside, all opposites healed into each other.

And then, last of all, a fourth dot, placed just below the lips. This dot is for silence, respect for the legacies left by the old ones in the place you are entering so that we come into knowing empty-handed. The sacred prefers not to be talked about but to be held as immanent, implicit, and contained.

Zhaozhou confirmed this natural reticence when he was asked a beautiful question: "What is the way of true ease?"

He replies, with gentle warning: "Pointing it out makes it uneasy."

A seed is deeply discreet about the great tree it holds in implicate form. Wisdom wisely guards living knowledge and its true ease from the ever-talking mind.

IT COMES DOWN ONLY ON US

"Don't skip leg day" is the wonderfully direct indigenous Australian way of saying, "Get your eye off yourself, get your act together, and turn up to the great work at hand."

"You can expect it to be a little costly," Tyson Yunkaporta drily comments,[8] which is to say costly to any number of habits of self-indulgence. And in another of those slanted Tibetan lojong slogans, I find the echo of the small-print warning attached to all genuine care for Country, all acts of practical compassion: "Don't expect applause."

The "ask" that Country makes of us becomes the completeness of how it holds us. That last white ochre dot, placed just under the ever-talking mouth, brings not simply respect Law with it, but the immense holding power of the Earth that comes to meet us when we relinquish our grip on the self. All of Earth's creative power is vested in a profoundly quiet discretion, as are all grounds for approaching it with the deepest respect and gratitude. And that strong discretion makes sure of the strangest gift it offers we two-leggeds: "It comes down only on us."

It comes down as damage and suffering; it comes down as a gift; it comes down as responding; it comes down as waking up.

CODA: RECONCILE WITH THIS

Once, walking in Country with Uncle Max and a party of people belonging to the very worthy Australian initiative called Australians for Native Title and Reconciliation, which advocates for Aboriginal rights and supports First Nations voices and interests, he suddenly stopped and said, "You know, I don't hold with this word *reconciliation*. How can there be reconciliation if there has never been a relationship in the first place?" Then he bent down and picked up a small handful of earth at his feet and held it out, saying, "I just tell both mobs, 'Reconcile with this.'"

After a moment, he added, "You won't need any 'reconciliation' after that."

His words echoed in every heart with the undeniable truth that the brutality of the colonizer toward the colonized is no relationship; it is a pointed refusal of one. Uncle Max's words that day were not said angrily, just said straight. What's the implication?

In his outstretched handful of earth lies the need to acknowledge and apologize for the wrongs of colonialism and to begin a genuine relationship of equals, based less in shame than in desire to learn and share life, for in the work of deep adaptation we save each other.

And in that handful of earth are words that do not state, argue, or refuse anything at all, but silently raise the inarguable fact that here, too, as Uncle Max said, "there has never been a relationship in the first place." The purely survivalist ethos expressed in, Get through as best you can, get away with the most you can, is a form of living by damage. "Mutually save, mutually save" is the logic of the relational ethos that lies at the heart of the Aboriginal culture that lies inside this Earth.

Our human world is fractured along a thousand excruciating lines. It begins with the split in our minds between the Earth and the self, fracturing complexly from there: the slow-motion collapse of the biosphere; the avalanche of extinctions; the yawning gulf between rich and poor; the less than fully human status accorded any perceived "other" in terms of race, gender, religion, and sexual preference. And on it goes, the split that goes on splitting all lines of the kinship that holds things together. A mending is long overdue.

Might a climate cataclysm be the greatest opportunity ever offered to our species to reconcile and walk a path that harmonizes with this living Earth? This is deep adaptation in the fullest sense. One mending of this split equally mends all.

"It comes down only on us." If our species manages to reconcile our relationship with the great Earth in a way that has deep time as its basis, the contesting differences between all "mobs" that comprise humanity will have been obliged to reconcile countless moments of difference on that path. And going through the difficult, testing transition of such deep adaptation together will have healed us as much as it may salvage and regenerate an accommodating, flourishing biosphere.

The koan of ecocrisis resolves as we and the Earth heal each other, transforming a deeply entrenched, domineering contempt for the Earth into a shared mind, shared body, and shared awakeness.

For "It is the literal body of the Earth, this Buddha."

stacked in stone
the vein of time

火

7

THIS FIRE IS A PATH

If you want to know what will happen in spring,
the winter plum blossoms simply do not know.

—HONGZHI

A person bathing in the great ocean uses all the waters that empty
into it.

—MAZU

The kinds of fire on Earth:

Wildfire, ignited by lightning strikes and vulcanism, endemic to this Earth;

Domesticated fire, for warmth, light, cooking, agriculture, creating the means of shared human life;

Feral fire, the new, unthinkable, unapproachable, nonsurvivable, habitat-simplifying megafire as a consequence of unearthing and burning fossil fuels;

Intelligent fire or *cool fire*, the cultural burning practice widely used by indigenous peoples, not just to moderate wildfire risk, but to lovingly regenerate the life of Country for both human and more-than-human flourishing;

Plus, one more: *human fire*, that of mind awake and ablaze in the undivided nature of this reality. This is the mind explored throughout this book, as is the fertile us-two that this mind can forge against the ecological and social tragedy of a profoundly disrupted climate. A testable, durable resilience rests in keen awareness of the vulnerability we all share—all beings, one body—together with a willingness to temper vulnerability's most panicked judgments into the intelligence of not-knowing, bending and moving with the way that everything moves *together*.

An old Torres Strait Islander once put Tyson Yunkaporta right, explaining that his effort should be just to "get my eye off myself, share freely, and it will all be taken care of." This beautifully expresses the spirit of Country, the mind of cool fire that trusts the many hands and eyes all over the "body" of the place where we are. They are all attentive and capable of taking care, with none heroically "doing" things and no one expecting applause.

TENDER

As we've seen, this mind that realizes the whole Earth as medicine is tender at heart. Deep adaptation is its natural bent, and not-knowing its genius for intimacy. As Polish writer Olga Tokarczuk said in her acceptance speech for the 2019 Nobel Prize in Literature, "Tenderness personalizes everything to which it relates, making it possible to give it a voice, to give it the space and the time to come into existence, and to be expressed."

It is thanks to tenderness that the trees can inform our minds and the language of Country can inform our dreams. With tenderness we can go down inside ourselves and come up in everything, alive! As Tokarczuk goes on to say,

Tenderness is deep emotional concern about another being—its fragility, its unique nature, and its lack of immunity to suffering and the effects of time. Tenderness perceives the bonds that connect us, the similarities and sameness between us. It is a way of looking that shows the world as being alive, living, interconnected, cooperating with, and codependent on itself.[1]

Deep adaptation is a kind of conscientization into this mind that is tender toward the planet. Such a mind breaks the culture of silence in which the Earth has been considered mute and inert, a natural object of domination and oppression. Such conscientization, in any context, raises a finely awake critical consciousness, which the late Brazilian educator and philosopher Paulo Freire (1921–1997) saw as priming the ability to intervene in reality in order to change it.

But this is no standing-over kind of mind. The genius of Freire's pedagogy for raising literacy in oppressed communities was to work hard and humbly to know nothing in advance, so as to discover and move together with the community's genius for learning that was already at hand. Close to the end of his life, Freire was asked, "What is the most important thing of all?" He is said to have replied, "It is the beautiful daily struggle to be congruent." This kind of tenderness is the modest, receptive face of love, the most self-relinquished form of wakeful understanding.

Congruent implies a perfect fit, one thing completely conforming to another. What would it mean for human beings to completely conform with the Earth? Each of Freire's words are equally important—the process is beautified by its struggle and must be as consistently alive to us as the word *daily* suggests. The word *practice* might also do as well. What calls us into such a beautiful and daily kind of struggle for congruence is left open by Freire, but right now, as explored in every page of this book, the Earth is making the great matter pretty plain.

A monk asks Zhaozhou, "What is the fact for which I must accept responsibility?"

Zhaozhou answers, "Though you search to the ends of time, you'll never single it out."

Zhaozhou offers both deep reassurance and the beautiful daily struggle at once here. The wondrous Earth that embraces all things may not be answerable to such questions. Her seamless state of being has not even a speck of "purpose" to be found. But we are rapidly finding that we are answerable to her nevertheless. Can the master be telling us that only if I can legitimately find the beginning or end to "me" will I ever be able to find a beginning or end to that which I must accept as "my responsibility"? The climate crisis makes it plain that you can never single yourself out from the Earth; not-knowing mind confirms this with every breath.

If this sounds impossibly daunting, remember that once you manage to let a koan bend your mind a little, things actually start looking oddly more straightforward. Think of Zhaozhou's question as just one more access point into the wonderful form of adult play that is koan mind, which loosens the strictures of consciousness that have not been serving us particularly well. It's an invitation to learn at last that we can approach and tenderly meet the reality that we are, and the Earth is. Like all great play, this is at once fun, imaginative, enlivening, deeply satisfying, and entirely sober and serious.

The ancient practice of cool fire in Country provides a case study of what the activation of deep adaptation might look like. And the practice of such an action of deep adaptation can seek only to turn things while turning intimately *with* things.

THE PRACTION

Filmmaker, musician, and educator Victor Steffensen is the author of *Fire Country: How Indigenous Fire Management Could Help*

Save Australia. He is a highly skilled holder of indigenous cultural burning practices, knowledge that is bred in the bones in a country that too easily burns. Steffensen is a descendant of the Tagalaka people from the Gulf Country of North Queensland. Two old lawmen gave him his fine-grained training in the subtle conversation with Country that is conducted through the judicious cultural use of fire. While training him, they also inadvertently endowed him with the neologism *praction* when referring to *practice*.[2] This beautiful coinage, its graceful dissolving of *practice* into *action*, is a gift for our urgent times that can help us reverse the disastrous course we're set ourselves on.

Recall Yanguan's sudden call to "bring me the rhinoceros fan," uttered to test his attendant, who replies, perhaps naively, "I can't. It's broken." Is he still in the mind of a separate self, elaborately extracted and carved out of the living whole? "Then bring me the rhinoceros!" says Yanguan. No one will ever "explain" a rhinoceros, here in its full, nonnegotiable presence and unrepeatable character. The mind of exploitative use of the Earth, that broken model of what we are here for, must be replaced by a mind more closely shared with the Earth—which is to say, it is immediately time to bring back the whole, live rhinoceros, head and horns complete. And inseparable from you.

The "praction" of using a cool fire to moderate fire danger and regenerate the life of Country is a pointer to how we might respond to the provocation Yanguan laid down before his attendant more than a thousand years ago. Our challenge in these times of a rapidly overheating planet is to wake with the spirited energy and obduracy of the mystery here named "rhino." To do so would be to prompt awareness of the fire that runs through this mysterious Earth seamless with this self, and thus to kindle deep adaptation and regeneration.

Practice is Zen's cool fire, its way of gradually waking up into "Mutually save, mutually save." Praction, then, can be understood as the regenerative power of practice actively realized and rippling out through human hands and eyes and into the world. And into Country, this vast compact of "We save each other" that has formed humbly and respectfully in tandem with the Earth. For what kind of practice is worth a moment's thought if it stops short of actualizing the wisdom it awakens?

Praction is conscientization that takes its lead from the Earth. It is a path of lifting the oppressive weight of the judging mind and letting Earth herself speak and be heard. What shifts might be inspired, what unexpected, rhinoceros-strength refusal of further bad human behavior might occur if we take a strong stand on the ground together with others who share a fierce love for the Earth, to collectively listen our way into action congruent with her?

LIGHTING A COOL FIRE

Fire praction in Country requires a state of mind that is considered and considerate enough to activate people, Country, and culture through shared learning and understanding. Such an activation can make the land happy again, in all its beings, from grasses and insects, to bushes and birds, to trees and forest communities, and even to clouds and waterways. "Everything benefits at the same time and in consideration of each other," writes Steffensen. "When the praction activates everything to move together, it becomes living knowledge."[3]

It Is the not-knowing mind that senses how everything moves together and activates human congruence with Country. Praction is action that is alive and unconfined, timeless and unhurried, because it is born from something ageless—like Country, like undivided reality. And such a relational ethos is not time-harried; it *grows* time.

"You have to walk the Country to read it," Steffensen advises, in order to pick up "the knowledge indicators poking out everywhere."[4] This means standing on the ground and noticing; touching and being touched. You "read the grasses by hand," he says, to feel for the exact balance of moisture and dryness that says yes to a cool fire, which yields the "good white medicine smoke" that radiates quietly out to a predictable distance and then peters out at a precisely anticipated point. A cool fire does not climb into high branches or *ever* touch the sacred upper world of the canopy. It will be cool enough to walk on barefoot soon after burning. And all the more-than-human creatures are able to make a safe exit while the fire burns and can soon return for the pickings—the stimulated regrowth, the renewed flowering.

Steffensen writes that to shift the paradigm and open minds we must "deliver the message gently," just as a cool fire does, in fact. "Getting angry doesn't work. It is important to be patient and allow for the understanding of others."[5] But this relaxed gaze that enables one to read "a language coming from Country that only trained eyes could see" flows only when "the land is the boss and tells us what to do" and when to do it.

Cultural fire training such as Steffensen proposes must meet the hardened views of fire management officials and the regulatory strictures of official "fuel hazard reduction" schedules. Steffensen laments that "the spirituality of the knowledge" can't flow easily into the existing categories of bureaucratic systems, for these categories are "tools of gain, of owning," and ancestral "knowledge fields" can't be owned, only shared.[6]

Among many salutary stories in his book, Steffensen shares that of a time when officers from the National Parks and Wildlife Service came for an indigenous culture fire workshop. I find in it a resonant teaching of how to apply the cool fire of koan mind to activating a healing change in an obdurate human world, set in its damaging ways. Even before the officers arrived at the workshop, they had issued strict edicts along the lines of: Alright, you can do a burn in this area but it will have to be in one-square-meter areas. And the one-square-meter areas have to be completely burned, nothing left half-done.

What? How can you possibly have an indigenous burn in one-square-meter sections? There were endless additional requirements issued in advance of the occasion that was technically dedicated to learning something outside the frame of white-fella knowledge.

Steffensen goes on to talk about how the "little bosses," as he calls them, having advanced some distance down the path of agreeing that there *was* something to learn here, are typically thrown right back to their former stance the moment the big boss man comes around. And then begins the painfully delicate process of trying to teach entrenched authority figures that, yes, some kind of indigenous knowledge may have value and be permitted to be demonstrated.

There's no distributed authority being found and shared in a stand-over posture of mind. Such a posture is founded in bad faith. Just as koan mind opens by trusting your own essential nature to realize itself, minds open best to their own genius of learning when learning is dignified as arising in all of its participants.

The cool fire demonstration finally went ahead, but only when a final, very self-important obstacle is met. This happened when the big boss man said to Steffensen, "I have just realized this definitely cannot go ahead." Why? "You can't wear shoes like that," he was informed. They had to be full-covered shoes, otherwise the burning couldn't go ahead. Victor was wearing the same soft, open shoes he has worn for every cultural fire he has ever managed across the decades. It was a stalemate until Steffensen mildly suggested, "What about I just sign a piece of paper that says I take full liability for myself?"[7]

With this, the big boss man at last gave way. Steffensen signed a grubby piece of paper on the hood of a car, and off they went.

Once permission was granted, the fire demonstration was revelatory. The work of transformation came from the Earth herself, drawing people from contestation into love and freedom. The people witnessing the cultural burn found themselves drawn into its close intensity. They fell in love with the sense of being freed from an old system that no longer works, and they felt a dawning recognition that an absurd load had slipped off their shoulders. Their faces lit up. "They become free," as Steffensen puts it. The main boss actually said at the end of the burn that he felt himself "grow free from the side of himself that was deprived of the truth, and of freedom that comes from the land." The cool fire proved to be a demonstration of an intricate interrelatedness shared with all the trees and bushes and grasses and creatures *and* every single human being present—like a koan breaking open.

Everybody found themselves sharing smiles in all directions by the end. They left with the sense that "the safest thing you can have in Country when burning is a living knowledge." This is interbeing in action, the very process of deep adaptation. "When the praction is activating everything to move forward together, it becomes living knowledge. . . . When that is activated, you can relax and deeply enjoy so many of those moments."[8]

Exposed to something like a cool fire, minds grow sharp and stay sharp, keened by the kind of attention essential to a deeply interwoven, nonlinear mind that can move with the subtle changes of eternal yet living Country. "And the land shows you the knowledge is true," writes Steffensen. It's an us-two, as the authority flows through the praction both ways with the Earth. "Once people get the idea, they can be left to continue the praction on their own country," he adds. "The land will keep teaching you even when the old people are gone."

Time seems so short to turn things around, but "Country creates time, the time you need to hear what is wanted," he writes.[9] And it also eases dissonance along with the torment of feeling powerless. Steffensen reassures us that "in navigating the never-ending journey, trust the question is trying to answer itself through you." We must learn "to sit and walk on the land, enter that mysterious space, and . . . entrust the question to the land's ability to answer."

Why? Because "walking the land is walking beyond ego mind."[10]

TALKING WITH THE EARTH

The world teems and buckles, ruptures and regenerates, and we move with it, offering what we can to nudge it toward healing. In the empty world, which is not separate from the roiling one, there is no forcing and no one to force. There is suffering, but it turns into the nerve to care deeply.

In the great fires of 2019 and 2020, those vast pyrocumulonimbus clouds towering over our heads crackled with thunder and spat fire-created drops of rain as we made final moves to flee and take shelter with friends. Under that apocalyptic skyscape I took a moment to attend to two final things. One was to lay out the zafus and zabutons in the meditation hall, as if summoning the spirit of all the many people who had ever sat in that hall and loved and taken care of it—a kind of votive offering to the weather gods as they debated our fate in deciding the direction the fire winds would turn in. The other was to take a moment to seek personal counsel from the Earth that mothers us, something I'd learned to do decades before in the company of the remarkable Wiradjuri elder Minmia, otherwise known as Auntie Maureen Smith:

Find a place that wants you to sit down on the ground. Take your time before easing your fingertips a little way into the earth, and then, when you feel the connection, speak your name out loud, saying, "This is your daughter/son [name], talking with you, Mother." Take a moment for the question that needs to be asked to arrive in your heart, then speak it out loud and wait for the return touch, the unexpected words that sound in your own heart.

My question that moment for the Earth arose from sheer exhaustion and sorrow that had all but replaced several months of mounting fear: "What do you need me to know about this?"

Her reply came in its own time with a slight buzz in my hands and a jolt to my heart: "Your suffering with me is my care for you."

It made unhesitating, koanlike sense. Exactly to the extent we hold back from suffering with the Earth, we stay blind to all that is offered in her "my care for you." The reality of "mutually save" springs from a willingness to completely share one vast vulnerability. It covers us, like wings.

There can be no flinching from the plain fact that we are to endure a great suffering with the Earth, which we ourselves have set in motion.

At every point in that perilous moment of megafire—including when I came back a day later and found our corner of the valley blessedly untouched by fire—the deeply consoling embrace of "I'm all yours" was confirmed in the words that Country gave me. To admit how sharply we suffer the wounding of the Earth in our own bodies lets something hard and scared in us soften and be held as it transforms into the mutual caring that is alive in Country.

ACCEPT ALL OFFERS

Uncertainty has great value when you turn toward it with not-knowing. Such a turn moves us toward greater intimacy with what is unfolding, making it a tender, playful move. That

Zen practice is itself a form of serious adult play becomes less surprising when you consider how games and play depend on rules, which are essentially a restriction of choice. In zazen, as in play, a less constrained, choiceless awareness opens your gaze to offers that a defensive, picking-and-choosing mind can't see. It is actually the rigor of Zen practice that raises everything to a state of play.

Any seriously undertaken work is play in the deepest sense. It might seem paradoxical that the very thing that most quickens the playful edge of the mind and upward tilt of spirit is the absolute gravity of the matter at hand: personal mortality, species extinction, and planetary ruin. "Play" inheres in the rigorous, testing path of discovery, which depends on an imaginative willingness to recognize just what is needed within a highly restricted space.

Play, by nature, expects the unexpected and is ready to discern and catch the offer of each moment. It undoes whatever we try to lay on the moment, for that is destined to miss the moment. All suppositions are up for testing. In play, time becomes elastic, just one more element to shape, intensify, and use—more like a child's sense of time, which is stretchy, available, and rich. This is the inherently playful side of the intelligence of emptiness.

Responding to a koan calls up the dragonish creative energy described in the first hexagram of the I Ching, "The Creative"— the electrically charged, arousing force of a spring thunderstorm. With koans, it becomes entirely possible to call up the whole great world in its minute particularities. The whole world is then at your disposal, so you can respond with an abundant economy of means. Here it is! Responding before thought can jump in— how is that not play? No wonder great, reassuring gusts of laughter often come from the Zen interview room, where you meet the master face to face in the light of your koan. This is laughter that can roll away the boulder and release us from the grave we make of this self.

Think of climate activism as a heightened form of play, the same way that practice is a profound form of play with your own life. All undertakings as serious as play are like the way a wave falls: it can't be predetermined; its rules provide the structure for chaos, and so it is as inexhaustible as clouds, as flowing as water cascading in waves. And it is alive, not doing your bidding, on the edge of risk. Japanese calligraphy master and Zen teacher, author, and translator Kaz Tanahashi says of the mind at play in brushwork that if it pleases the eye, it is not yet dangerous enough. Once more, the path to resilience lies in willing vulnerability and in pushing past the presumed safety of knowing.

Accepting all offers and finding the "yes!" that can keep rising to meet the dangerous, oblique offers being thrown at us by an unfolding crisis is a profound move to make. It means equally accepting the offering of suffering, loss, sickness, old age, and death. Taking unavoidable suffering on as an interesting if difficult offer opens the way to realizations that a neurotic resistance to suffering can never perceive.

FAULT AND NO FAULT

As we saw in chapter 5, "It's my fault," an appropriately dangerous-seeming koan, is one we must allow to take us up as the gift of our peculiar time. True conscientization cannot proceed from a mind that judges "right" in advance, and so is poised to find "wrong."

Of course, we share in the trillions of grievous acts and decisions that are beyond our individual reach, many of them adopted despite the heart's strong protest at the obviously appalling consequences. The pocket-size koan "It's my fault" has the power to critically examine the constriction within our hearts while also, paradoxically, beginning to ease it.

"It's my fault" is immediately ridiculous at a planetary level... but wait—how is it not my fault, and the tree's fault, the sea's fault, and the fault of the very nature of the great wide Earth, the sun, the moon and the stars? If this self cannot finally be separated out to stand grandiosely alone from anything at all, how then can "fault" be separated out? Yes, there are malevolent forces perpetrating the collective crime that is climate collapse, but when you accept that all of this arrives together with you and is inseparable from you, strangely enough the walls don't close in on you, they begin to fall away.

Not only does "fault" cease to be what draws and starts to narrow the gaze, but "my" grows hard to hold onto as well, along with "me" as opposed to "you," in whatever form. By taking personal responsibility, it grows harder to find either the one who must be blamed or the sense of being so very right that there's little else to see. The fire that runs through all things is unimpeded by this thing called "me," revealing and liberating what lives prior to "fault." In moving beyond "me," beyond the narrowly partisan self, a more fine-grained field of awareness opens. We can begin to notice what the whole situation is needing us to notice, and to recognize ourselves in those words of Thomas Aquinas, "Capable of the universe are your arms as they move with love." Suffering ripens into discovering our own true face in the other, in no other at all.

Dogen's path beyond "mistake" has the simplest of instructions: "Do not leave this place abruptly." Beyond faultfinding lies the unhurried, open response; without leaving the demon world you walk in the buddha world. By practicing to teach your own demons to sit in zazen (to learn to come safely apart), the demons of planetary crisis—panic, rage, conspiracy mind, impossible grief—can begin to intelligently unpick the fear hiding behind the anger, the frightened love trapped in the grief, the heart-opening prayer for help energized within the lunacy. This is to realize the whole Earth and all that is here as the medicine of transformation.

Being present to our precarious moment has multiple time-lines, all of them alive in you as you sit and contemplate the vast dilemma. Here and now, the sound of birds, the touch of air, the life of trees, warm companions—so much to touch and be touched by, to do and to celebrate, so much to dance with! Suffering is here too, along with sorrow, anger, and grief. None are turned away.

Going wider, to the many currents of our shared historic time in all its pathos, tragedy, and idiocy, we can also recognize ourselves as inseparable from the emergent field. And in each such moment, going deeper, we can't help but touch the no-time that is so clearly where being arrives, breath by breath, clear as a bell, just as long as we don't leave this place abruptly, which is to say, to not leap to conclusions. This is where a crazed and improbable instruction like "then bring me the rhinoceros" turns sane, original, and complete. It walks alive in each of us, opening its eyes in every moment and becoming a perfectly reasonable suggestion.

Consider the words of Jesuit priest, poet, and peace activist Daniel Berrigan (1921–2016), who was famous as one of the draft card–burning Catonsville Nine. Later, as part of the Plowshares movement, he was among the activists who took sledgehammers to a missile silo and damaged the warhead there, spilled pig's blood on the floor, and deliberately set off alarms, then waited to be arrested and do some jail time. I have heard that Berrigan's advice for resolving an impossibly formidable problem like a world infested with nuclear arms was, "Start with the impossible, then proceed calmly toward the improbable."

In truth, where else is there to start? As long as we stay frozen in "impossible," harm is freely perpetrated and its plausible deniability persists unchallenged. It feels wiser to "proceed calmly toward the improbable" with all that we are, led by the joy of pure being. Learning to do the impossible is not unlike learning to ride a bicycle. Somehow, we learn to put our faith in that impossibility and sail forth on such a fragile apparatus in an astonishing way; or learn to crawl, or to forgive. Every human body is in many ways impossible, yet look how wonderfully well they accomplish the improbable, as a daily matter.

As every koan confirms, the force of "impossible" and "improbable" is needed to open the way. Koans, like any valuable crisis, offer us no choice but to push past the impasse of ourselves to where there are no impediments (and never were). There's only us, with our fear taken in hand and that strange new gift of fearlessness already responding, already "doing what cannot be done."

A BUTTERFLY FLIES UP

Let's look into the tenderness of this way of responding through a disarming-seeming koan:

> When the wind blows, the downy willow seed floats
> away.
> Rain beats on the peach blossoms. A butterfly flies up!

How mysterious, how improbable are our lives and this world. Both lines of this two-part koan take the measure of cause and effect, of one thing becoming another, but they engage subtly different ways of seeing into emptiness.

Downy willow seed, so light and so fluffy—even the merest thought of a breeze has it already flying away. It's as if such a downy seed premeditates the wind, manifesting a state of mutual readiness. This is not unlike the receptiveness of nonthinking or Dogen's "the thought of no-thought," the unmitigated heartmind response that comes forth before self-referencing thought can step in to fashion a safe holdout. It is as seamless as "wind blows . . . willow seed floats." In this seed-wind moment, as in reality, there's nothing static, settled, or independently existent, including each one of us. We're nothing but one mysterious *responding*, one flow of universe, Earth, events, beings, actions, reactions, feelings, thoughts, and realizations.

Call and response mutually arise. When my daughter was tiny, I would find one foot already out of bed and on the floor with the first murmur from her cot. I couldn't separate the smallest first sounds of a baby's hunger from something deep in my sleeping state that was already poised. This empty, open, mutual tissue of being lives earlier than thought. And while such an affinity can't be premeditated, we can practice making ourselves as exquisitely *available* to it as possible.

Critical awareness of how to help shift the dial of convulsive change toward favoring life will come alive in a mind more open to moving with the ceaseless flow of reality. To presume is to step out of that informing current, while not-knowing moves with it.

Nothing stays the same. Is there really a "next" when you go all the way to where this koan draws us? Our wishes and plans must accord with the fact that no final state is to be found anywhere in reality. There can be no ultimate judgment, as nothing is ever finished (or categorically "begun"). And yet within our human lifespan we are asked to distinguish better from worse, nonharming from harming, and to choose actions that help shape events to flow in the most beneficial direction.

"Rain beats on the peach blossoms. A butterfly flies up!" Feel for a shift to something more incisive here. You can't *not* feel with the butterfly, with the blossoms, with the pelting rain. Blossoms are fragile, delicate, butterflies too, and likewise human bodies. And then comes the hard, wet rain, and seamless with that, the fresh thing: a butterfly flies up!

Just for a moment, consider: was that a butterfly blossoming or a peach blossom flying up in the pelting rain? The dream of the Earth has the character of one boundless, free interchange, while the call of the Earth on us is to rise up appropriately and exactly, guided by and helping to guide this wondrous matter.

The climate crisis is dire. But in its midst, "a butterfly flies up," a surge of responsive energy born out of what is pressing on us at this time. What instinctively flies up in you to counter the forces beating on the delicate web of life, the fragile biosphere? The mutuality that holds this vast flung universe together, and is what has made the Earth self-healing up to now, is a power that flows also by nature as us—when we hold our considerable powers of disruption sufficiently in check. There's no traceable agency creating ecological balance; no one knows how the impossible is done. But meanwhile, improbably, it happens all the time, and in endlessly fresh ways. Rain beating ruinously on fragile peach blossoms becomes a butterfly strongly flying up, alive! We can take refuge in this indivisible affinity of call and response.

"With no walls in the mind, no walls and therefore no fear" is a translation of one of the most potent lines in the Prajna-paramita (meaning "Perfection of Wisdom") Heart Sutra. Awakening has no-fear in it. "Don't be afraid to be afraid. Don't be appalled to be appalled," Daniel Berrigan is said to have counseled. We actually have no choice. Facing a planetary crisis, we cannot indulge being afraid or appalled. Nothing that matters was ever saved by turning away in shame, fear, or disgust. To not respond to the defining crisis of Earth and humanity in our times would be to surrender the very gift of life. Shocked, surprised, battered perhaps, yet rising up in response to the pressure, which is the gift of being here now.

This kind of responsiveness is heightened in Zen practice. Self-nature is one continuous responding, but not-knowing brings forth its intelligence. To practice not-knowing is to work skilfully with the grain of what is emerging. We each have our own distinct part in discerning and shaping the form it takes. The one who responds in this potent but noncoercive way is what Linji challenges us to find in ourselves: "The true person of no rank." His famous phrase calls up the one who has no name, no insignia, no distinguishing marks, no expectation of applause. The true person has no one looking on and is hard to distinguish from just what is happening. They have access to the most intuitive countermoves to the coercive, ruinous, power-over mind.

DOING WHAT CANNOT BE DONE

The tiny nectar-sipping hummingbirds flitting between flowers must find ten times their body weight in nectar every day to meet their super-high metabolic rate. They do so with a ripe, ready intent that is highly focused and responsive in every one of their immediate, meticulous movements, but nothing that is driven, obsessive, or compulsive. Is this why our eyes love them so much? Nevertheless, human beings seem saddled with the strange compulsion to always be *doing* rather than *being*.

You can study not-doing in a busily moving stream; in every single ripple is that sense of being completely in agreement with what is, an accuracy earlier than choice. Go around this bit of grass, rejoin up over here, and then mosey along before toppling over those few rocks . . . one long prayer of flowing with what is. One timeless appropriate response.

Meditation gradually grows in us a tolerance for what is actually happening, without the self-punishing holding-back, less clouded by the constant, shifting preferences of an uneasy self. For if such a self persists in the foreground of your sitting, your meditation becomes painful, absurd even. Instead, there's a depth of contentment open to us in zazen, the sense of easing into the blessed state of wanting nothing or very little at all. This is seating yourself closer to the still point of all that's flowing through life.

Freeing ourselves up from the small wants heightens sensitivity to the cries of the Earth and other beings, and bestows a greater ability to respond in the most natural, elemental, and immediately helpful way. Expect to find this painful. Expect to find it joyous, too. And expect to find it ordinary. Luckily, ogres are here to help with this.

There was once an ogre who lived under a bridge and would pop out whenever anyone came in their cart rumbling toward him. He would jump out in front of them, barring their way to the bridge, and say, "Stop! Say a turning word for me or you can't go over my bridge and I will eat you!" Those encountering the ogre would get very flummoxed by this—a bit like the silence that often yawned in the wake of Yunmen's questions, such as, "Then what is this self?" or, "Now, what is your light?" Many people got eaten.

On one occasion, however, a farmer came along with his heavy-laden cart and simply said to the ogre, "But I've got to get all these vegetables to market!" The ogre waved him through with an "On you go!"—the most simple, ordinary, and fully earthed response, on both sides of the matter. That's what so easily gets missed in the drive for control or preferred outcome, or when we flummox ourselves into silence because somebody or some threatening-looking situation is demanding, "What's at the heart of the matter here?" or asking, "What can you offer to help clear the way?"

Let naturalness carry you. Just be ordinary, and you cannot help but land on what is true and congruent, beyond reproach.

NAVIGATING WILD WATER

I once heard a whitewater expert describing a class V river:

A class I river: you can go canoeing, no problem. A class VI river: don't even think about it. And a class V river? The only way you can go down that river is if you're confident you know how to find and follow the through line, the safest way through the rapids. The through line is not an outcome, it's the way through a constantly changing flow.

The world is in a class V river now, wouldn't you say? Savage rocks ahead and on either side of us could destroy our boat, and fierce whirlpools could swallow us whole. As with Country, we must learn to read conditions beyond the noise of "There's a rock that will shred our boat!" or "That whirlpool will plunge us in headfirst, our fragile boat sucked under!"

To find the subtle through line in a class V river, you must be able to read all the small, telling details. If you miss them, they can spin you toward the big dangers. It is crucial, our whitewater expert said, not ever to fix attention on the truly big obstacles and dangers because they will magnetize your attention and draw your fear to only them, and that way you'll miss the subtle, salvific through line discovered only when you stay fully aware of the *entire* river.

Responding cannot be mapped in advance of discerning what is immediately happening right where we are. Like setting a cool fire, effective moves of deep adaptation are and will be discovered only in the intimacy and intelligence grounded in not-knowing, not presuming. This is taking refuge in wild river, Country, human beings, threat of disaster . . . in precariousness itself.

And most important of all, our river-running expert advised: when looking for the through line, you are looking for it in concert with all the people in the boat. *All* the many eyes and hands are needed to find and stay in accord with the flow. A class V river is not an object to be fought or conquered in an act of personal heroism. There is relief in letting go the mind of being in militant opposition to reality and instead seeking to navigate the subtlety of its flow. It is the same in activism and collective action of any kind: to propose a single powerful enemy that must be overcome is to resource and strengthen and rivet all eyes on one, missing the perspective of the emergent field of circumstance. The great revelation of our practice is that in the deepest intimacy we can find with reality, there is no "other."

FOLLOW NATURE

The way of Zen offers a through line for action (as far as humanly possible) in concert with all others. Downy seed, floating wind, pelting rain, rising butterfly, seething river, fragile boat—you can't pry them apart. The sense of threatening otherness may be hard to abandon under pressure of our peril, but the softening of "otherness" *is* the clear way through the crisis. As Flora Courtois concisely puts it, "We don't get enlightened at all. Rather, we enlighten each moment with true attention and complete response." The field of emergence that we need to keep on enlightening opens here.

When Bashō (1644–1694) was asked what it is that a poet needs to know, he said, quite simply, "Learn from nature and follow nature." Earth's hallmark is her essential ecological coherence. Following that deep inner pattern, any complex situation is best approached as *the ecology of the circumstance*. If you look to the natural world you will always see your clearest self, for easy reference. Open, unopinionated, poised, already *ready*.

Such an ecological approach does not mentally separate things out and pin them down but perceives a constant field of emergence, an older order always giving way. The cosmos seems to like transcending itself in fiery cataclysmic transformations on occasion, but its more common creative move is one of transmutation: a slow and gradual responding within constraints to create increasing excellence of form and fitness within conditions, as one thing or state adapts in a coherent process of turning into something else. And at every point, this process of transmutation relies on yielding individual demands to intricate patterns of interdependence that are vast beyond reckoning.

Zen practice slowly mineralizes in our own bones some of these formative powers of the universe, none of them lacking fire—not just the cataclysmic coup de grâce of waking up, but equally the cool fire of patient endurance that transforms one state of being into another. All of which, together with this very body and mind, were implicit in the original fireball! Along with the entire shimmering field of emergence we call life on Earth.

THE SHIMMER

We know that the infinitely patient genius that is life persisted through at least 3.5 billion years to bring forth a brain that could conceive of and investigate the earliest unicellular beings it has evolved from. Every step and accident within that long expanse of time took place in intimate, creative tension with severe constraints, and with countless mutation experiments either rejected or accepted along the way. Just ask COVID-19 about this.

Life is one story. It is original, comprehensive, distributed, enjoyed, formative of every living being on Earth, and it takes everyone without exception as its amazed subject. Dharma, like Country, is the Earth and universe speaking this mystery directly in human terms. Deborah Bird Rose called life's vast play of mutuality "the shimmer"—this great, ongoing cycle of giving that is receiving, more subtle and far-reaching than anything we can think up or predict. She explored its play of "Yes!" as the powerful and brilliant "shimmer" of the biosphere. Think, for instance, about how flowering trees entice insects, birds, possums, and fruit bats to the seductive shape, color, and smell of their flowers and fruit, rewarding the opportunistic thieves with an extravaganza of high-value nutrients while exploiting their mobility to seed descendants far across the land.

The shimmer of life manifests as one great, profligate gift economy always bestowing an unthinkable explosion of infinitely varied life-forms. Who, when it comes right down to it, makes whom within this shimmer? And who enlightens whom as human beings wake up within the shimmer that originates in eternity?

Every breath in is a "yes" to the mutual deal between photosynthesis and our every breath out, with its release of carbon dioxide. Every breath we take in is a "yes" as well, to the wave of emergence out of deep time that we crest, for now.

But every alienated "no" that our actions on Earth speak dulls the shimmer and unmakes its ancestral power. This "no" rejects the allure of mutuality that calls us to take our part in multispecies care. This "no" stifles our expressive powers of love. If we were not so dulled by the illusion of standing apart, we'd be completing the gift cycle of the Earth more consciously and well. But across the warm and hospitable Holocene of the last ten thousand years, driven by fear, lack, envy, and impatience—and just because we could—we have ever more forcefully replaced Earth's idea of the gift with the human notion of the quick, totalizing grab.

Every koan is a precisely placed depth-charge to jolt human consciousness back into alignment with our one shared reality. Every koan asks, "Are you here where you are? Can you dare welcome yourself here?" For we find ourselves entirely welcome "here" exactly as far as we can welcome the precarious and interwoven nature of present reality as the given.

IT'S US

Everyone has a dog in the fight to reinvent the human being for the sake of the life of planet Earth.

I hope you can sense by now how much the not-knowing

honed by the Zen koan tradition opens us up to the possibility of a curious and seriously playful engagement with crisis—serious, yet mobile, alert, nose to the ground, imagination alight, intently alert, following the scent trail, discounting nothing of interest along the way, landing always with our feet on the ground. Not unlike a joyful dog! Proceeding this way is a delight: complete arrival in each step, and each step a fresh suggestion about what the next may be. One intuitively congruent move at a time occurring in countless forms and situations on the Earth—this is the way of deep adaptation.

Protests come when the social contract or the Earth covenant has been noticeably violated. The protesting heart mirrors the protesting Earth, which in turn mirrors our climate derangement. Protesting in the street confirms that I am not alone in my anger, which can be empowering and can ripple out to rouse whole communities into responsive action. And justifiable protest, clearly heard, creates a new, cohesive citizenry where only atomized individuals existed previously.

So, protest can help dislodge us from a one-inch heart. It's true we can be so used to the everyday nightmare that we lose our ability to wake up from it without the help of anger. But does the heat of anger transmute readily into living knowledge, in myself and in those not yet moved enough to care?

Yes, but only to a point. Anger motivated by what is completely clear and clean right to the bottom is rare. The nonnegotiable "No, this must stop!" is the first step toward ameliorating harm to the Earth and her beings, and this can build into a surge of empathic, compassion-fueled anger that knows clearly what must be opposed. Yet even righteous anger can get caught up in right and wrong. When we are so very right, we are already becoming wrong, especially since we're all so deeply entwined in one another.

When an Australian terrorist gunned down fifty-one

worshippers at two Christchurch mosques in 2019, it happened to be on the day and at the very hour of the School Strike for Climate Action, held in dozens of places in Australia and New Zealand and across the world. The march of children in Christchurch happened to be, in per capita terms, the largest on the planet. News of the atrocity that was committed at the mosque reached the students just as the march was ending, when they began to search for media coverage of their protest.

Immediately, a large group ran to the park nearest one of the sites of the tragedy. And what did they do? They began to perform a powerful *haka* to express their grief and solidarity, adopting the Maori way of conveying strength, authority, and deeply contained conviction. Media rushed cameras to cover this surprising, spontaneous eruption, but the girls performing the haka fiercely banned all cameras, saying, "Stop! No! This is *not* for the media!"

Later, one boy who was there reflected on the origins of this immediate impulse to pour "No! This must stop! We are with you!" into that formidable Maori ceremonial form that stamps the ground with Earth's returning dust and power. "I think the earthquake told us to dance," he said. He was referencing the massive 2016 earthquake that so devastated Christchurch's homes and civic buildings, liquefying the ground and causing large loss of life. Pressed to explain, he said that ruinous earthquake had transformed Christchurch into a true community, bringing down the walls of fear between its different races and religions and political groups. Earth's strong statement, reconciling people into one.

Later, Jacinda Ardern, then prime minister of New Zealand, addressed the devastated mourners with these simple words of complete embrace: "You are us." The commonplace "We're all in this together" is still subtly stranded in a mind of "You, comma, and me," but "You are us" catches separation in the act of healing itself back into wholeness.

A HEALING FIRE

To reach beyond our anger and fear, the force of love and community must be raised to meet the vast, immiserating events related to climate collapse. To any protest or political action consider adding the power of dance, music, singing, storytelling, improv, clowning, dreamwork, ritual, and all forms of art that draw us into one shared body-mind. Let the profound as well as the absurd be plainly seen in pointed conversations, and what is deathly grow inarguably plain to see. And never forget what silence can lend to acts requiring a memorable social eloquence. Mahatma Gandhi is said to have declared, "A protest that can be expressed through silence is the final word in artistic language." Silence can go beyond the withholding of consent to become eloquent "speech" in potent acts of publicly bearing witness, of silent shunning or shaming, and of open mourning.

Satire, farce, and other forms of humor can also trigger a massive change of heart. The old koan masters similarly used loud yelling, sudden movement, and even sharp slaps at times, together with gusts of great laughter—not in judgment but to get past their students' tightly held minds before thought could arrive in their defence. There's much to borrow from the improvisational mind of the koan tradition to trigger sorely needed tipping points in consciousness.

And let's not forget the joy that gets ignited whenever we overturn old suppositions to find the fresh, new perspective. Successful civil disobedience employs playful, symbolic, impassioned, and yet morally impeccable tactics. Many flexion points in history offer us examples of powerful direct action or example that managed to displace the same old same old, to allow a powerful, fresh alternative to manifest. A few examples:

- In the 1980s, supporters of Solidarity, the movement instigated by the Polish trade union, took to the streets to push their unplugged television sets around in baby carriages in the evening right at the time of the nightly news broadcast, to demonstrate their utter rejection of government-controlled media and heavily censored news.

• Beginning in the early 1990s, in an attempt to slow rapacious deforestation in their countries, Thai, Burmese, Cambodian, and later also Sri Lankan Buddhist monks began publicly performing the ceremonial ordination of carefully selected forest trees as monks, tying saffron cloths to their trunks and bestowing monastic vows so as to confer a sacred standing that would frequently succeed in making the loggers turn back.

• Throughout the 1990s, Maha Ghosananda, an elderly Cambodian Buddhist monk in the Theravada tradition, made many long, slow, dangerous pilgrimages through the war-ravaged villages of post–Khmer Rouge Cambodia. He was joined along the way by thousands, actively imparting skills of peace and reconciliation as he walked from place to place while also organizing the perilous work of removing landmines in a countryside that had at that time more landmines than people.

Deep adaptation is the great human art form now being asked of us to address the absurdity of civilizational suicide. We have no choice but to enter the work of reinventing the human being to be more fit for Earth's purpose, for the sake of what it is we love—which turns out to be for the sake of what love is.

In one sense, all art is already protest in its urgency to express the vital fullness of reality. Whether artful protest celebrates or chastises the world, whether it expresses a hymn of praise or a jeremiad of anger, such poetic nerve challenges willful blindness, cries out against lack, laments crushing excess, and denounces cruelty, as it brings forward what is of greatest value. Protest like this relieves, redeems, and heals. It takes a luminous, koanlike leap into the darkness to refuse complicity with living by damage.

When such awareness grows, artful protest can draw us further toward what may yet be discovered, is being discovered, and is available to be shared. Like a koan breaking open in a public way, something wonderful can result from creative civil disobedience that literally demonstrates a fresh and potent understanding, one that has had no place in collective thinking up to now. This can resolve impossible or improbable opposing forces in one collective gesture that leaves a strong indentation in consciousness.

As witnessed in Victor Steffensen's cool fire demonstration of care for Country, even when action is aimed at changing a political course that is far too set in its ways, the creativity of praction lies in refusing to classify or categorize, refusing to proclaim one's rightness or issue edicts. Instead, like a Zen koan, the praction of regeneration is entrusted to the cool fire of the not-knowing mind, continually at work on the koan of the ecocrisis by way of resolving Yunmen's great three-part koan: Medicine and sickness heal each other. The whole Earth is medicine. What then is this self?

A cool fire opens the way for true knowledge to come alive in us. It provides a ground that we can safely walk on, one that confirms our solidarity with one another and with all beings of the Earth.

In the end, what else is there to do on a jewel of a planet like this one? With the whiskers of the tiger and the heat of the tiger's breath brushing our most personal and original face, there are no other options.

CODA: TRULY, IS ANYTHING MISSING NOW?

All of the world's critically important work, undeterred by what may or may not happen next, gets done by ordinary people like us, with all our usual frailties and handicaps. Writer James Baldwin (1924–1987) could have been speaking of our times when he said that the sea incessantly rises, the light fails, lovers cling to each other, and children cling desperately to us: "The moment we break faith and cease to hold each other, the sea engulfs us, and the light goes out."[11]

But is there not also something we can hold onto in ourselves and as ourselves that mysteriously appears only when we relinquish ourselves?

Mazu, speaking from the heart of his times—which, like ours, were ravaged by war, hunger, persecution, and social collapse—rendered the matter plainly: "To advance from where you can no longer advance, and to do what can no longer be done, you must make yourself into a raft or ferryboat for others." No-self, the constantly refining reference point of not-knowing, is that ancient ferryboat. And it carries *you*.

He points to the strange nature of the freedom found in the midst of suffering, the resilience located within vulnerability, the companionship and joy established and set in motion in acts of sharing a fierce love for the Earth—the lotus that burns in the midst of fire. Mazu also declared, "The fruit of the Buddha way is this: Each circumstance you encounter constitutes the meaning of your life. When you understand that fully, your actions are unhindered by anything else. You respond according to the needs of the moment." Because with this realization you are fully this moment. There is no other, and no drag of success or failure.

The threat of extinction is now holding open the exquisite possibility of changing our human course with the speed of rising consciousness. Could this be simpler than any form of master plan? Earth suffers and bleeds as we suffer and bleed, so clearly something in us already shares what is needed and knows what to do. Climate collapse steadily obliges us to take a long and grueling path of deep inquiry that can sustain deep

THE WHOLE EARTH IS MEDICINE

adaptation, but luckily you cannot walk this pilgrimage without honoring the Earth and all who walk with you. Your feet press the ground, and the ground presses back. Your upright, bony body that walks the Earth is Earth-calibrated and gravity-informed at every point. It welcomes your feet as an act of communion—which it is. Your hands reach out and are touched by other hands, and you laugh out loud.

The surprising joy is that when we turn to the Earth, we each turn out to be what it needs. Hakuin Ekaku's "Song of Zazen" ends with these three resonant lines:

> Truly, is anything missing now?
> This very place is the Lotus Land,
> This very body, the Buddha.

In the *Extensive Record of Yunmen Wenyan*, a single phrase from that equally difficult time—equally full of our haunted, human sense of *lack*—is taken up as three variations on a theme. Like a piece of music, each variation opens the way to the great resolving chord of shared inquiry.

Xuefeng's words get it going: "Someone sitting next to a basket of food is starving to death. And someone sitting next to a flowing river is dying of thirst." Who is this blind and needlessly impoverished being? Any sense of the strangeness evoked by our Earth-alienated, self-estranged state of consciousness?

The Chan master Xuansha Shibei (835–908) takes it up next: "Such a person is sitting in a basket of food, and such a person is up to their neck in water." Open your eyes, it's all around us, we're sitting in what it is that we seek, swimming in it in fact! How wonderful! Truly, is anything missing now?

But Yunmen moves to close out even the slight gap still left in Xuansha's words: "Her whole body is food. Her whole body is water," he insists. Truly, there is nothing missing, nothing hidden, no lack, and no outside to this. It is not only ready to be given, it's already all that you are. What will you do with it, this very body, the Buddha?

We are as complete and resourced as this, whether awake to it or not. We can't separate ourselves from the one unstinting *give*—it's what we are. Yunmen's challenge, which effectively says, My whole body is food, my whole body is water, is a potent evocation of the bodhisattva spirit. I'm all yours. What's needed here?

As for this "great body"—who or what's left out when it's as wide and complete as this mind? Can we live this way without reservation? And does awareness not charge us with a fierce love for the Earth, fierce enough for what's needed? That playful, four-way conversation across the ages between Xuansha, Xuefeng, Yunmen, and us sees "problem" or "lack" all the way back to where it can no longer be excised out from one exacting manifest reality.

"A person bathing in the great ocean uses all the waters that empty into it," says Mazu. Just try sorting out the parts of an ocean! This great ocean of undivided reality is entirely at our disposal whenever we notice that *it is us!*

To throw yourself into that water, try starting with the always pointed, clarifying question, "What does this ask in the light of my death?" But as you relax more deeply into it at every point, you find the simplest question of all, utterly tender, at the radiant core of the not-knowing mind: "What would love do now?"

> unbroken horizon
> a lone swimmer
> enters the sea

NOTES

PREFACE

1. As cited in Emily Dickinson's letters by Anderson, Charles A., "The Conscious Self in Emily Dickinson's Poetry," *American Literature* 31 (3): 290-308.

INTRODUCTION: FIRE, RAIN . . . AND A RHINOCEROS

1. Bendell, Jem. "Deep Adaptation: A Map for Navigating Climate Tragedy." IFLAS Occasional Paper 2, July 27, 2018. See also for later iterations: https://jembendell.com/2019/05/15/deep-adaptation-versions/.
2. Merwin, W. S. From "The River of Bees," in *The Second Four Books of Poems*. Port Townsend, WA: Copper Canyon Press, 1993.
3. Adapted slightly from Cleary, Thomas. *The Blue Cliff Record*. Boston: Shambhala, 1977, 489. Note: Cleary renders the names in the Wade-Giles style of Chinese transliteration into English; I choose the more contemporary preference, to render them in the pinyin style.
4. Ikkyū, *Wild Ways: Zen Poems*, trans., ed., John Stevens (Buffalo, NY: White Pine Press, 2003), 26.

CHAPTER 1: WHAT IS THIS SELF?

1. Hall, Donald. *Life Work*. Boston: Beacon Press, 1993: 53-54.
2. Stockholm Declaration on the Human Environment, in *Report of the United Nations Conference on the Human Environment*. New York: United Nations, June 5–16, 1972. Available online.
3. Yunkaporta, Tyson. *Sand Talk: How Indigenous Thinking Can Save the World*. Melbourne, Australia: The Text Publishing Co., 2019, 20.

CHAPTER 2: PRECARIOUS

1. Ortega y Gasset, José. *Meditations on Hunting*. New York: Charles Scribner and Sons, 1972, 130.
2. Whitman, Walt. "Song of the Rolling Earth," in *Leaves of Grass*. Available online.
3. Hass, Robert. Epigraph quote for Section One, *Praise* (poems). New York: Ecco Press, 1999.

CHAPTER 3: A FIRE RUNS THROUGH ALL THINGS

1. Cleary, Thomas, trans. *Secrets of the Blue Cliff Record: Zen Comments by Hakuin and Tenkei*. Boston: Shambhala, 2002, 42.
2. Becket, Samuel. *The Unnameable*. London: Faber and Faber, 2010, 59.
3. Hinton, David. *China Root: Taoism, Ch'an, and Original Zen*. Boulder, CO: Shambhala, 2020, 49.
4. Salinger, J. D. "Teddy," *Nine Stories*. Boston: Little, Brown and Company, 1953.
5. Loeb Classical Library, "On the Universe," https://www.loe

bclassics.com/view/heracleitus_philospher-universe/1931/
pb_LCL150.477.xml.

CHAPTER 4: LIVING IN A HOUSE ON FIRE

1. Glück, Louise. "From the Japanese," *Poems 1962–2012*. New York: Farrar, Straus and Giroux, 1985, 195.
2. Rilke, Rainer Maria. *Letters to a Young Poet*, trans. M. D. Herter Norton. New York: W.W. Norton, rev. ed., 1954, 23.
3. Mackenzie, Michael and Anna Kelsey-Sugg. "Freezing water and a shark encounter helped Ross Frlylinck to forge a powerful relationship with nature." Life Matters, ABC RN, Nov. 8, 2021. https://www.abc.net.au/news/2021-11-09/ross-frylink-craig-foster-cold-water-swimming-in-south-africa/100584846.
4. Rose, Deborah Bird. "Double-Death." The Multispecies Salon. www.multispecies-salon.org/double-death/.

CHAPTER 5. THE LOTUS IN THE MIDST OF FLAME

1. Verse translated by Robert Aitken and Yamada Koun and used largely in this form throughout the Diamond Sangha.
2. Snyder, Gary. "Just One Breath: The Practice of Poetry and Meditation." *Tricycle*, Fall 1991. https://tricycle.org/magazine/just-one-breath/.
3. Yampolsky, Philip B., trans. "Orategama I," in *The Zen Master Hakuin: Selected Writings*. New York: Columbia University Press, 1971, 37.
4. Mahdawi, Arwa. "Cyclist asks judge to show compassion to Brisbane driver who tried to run him down." *The Guardian*, Dec. 26, 2022. www.theguardian.com/australia-news/2022

/dec/06/cyclist-asks-judge-to-show-compassion-to-bris
bane-driver-who-tried-to-run-him-down.

CHAPTER 6: THE FIRE, EARTHED

1. Yunkaporta, Tyson. *Sand Talk: How Indigenous Thinking Can Save the World*. Melbourne, Australia: The Text Publishing Co., 2019, 29.
2. *Songline* refers to the tracks of Aboriginal Dreaming creation ancestors that crisscross the continent, leaving sacred and secret-sacred sites in their wake. Songlines are sung up (kept active, alive, and in the mind) through ceremony, art, and multilayered Dreaming stories.
3. Yunkaporta, 112.
4. Hinton, David, trans. *No-Gate Gateway: The Original Wu-Men Kuan*. Boulder, CO: Shambhala, 2018, xii–xiii.
5. Hinton, 132.
6. Mowaljarlai, David, with Jutta Malnic. *Yorro Yorro: Everything Standing Up Alive: Rock Art and Stories from the Australian Kimberley*. Broome, Australia: Magabala Books, 1993, 53-54.
7. Mowaljarlai and Malnic, 47.
8. Yunkaporta, 29.

CHAPTER 7: THIS FIRE IS A PATH

1. Tokarczuk, Olga. "The Tender Narrator." Dec. 7, 2019, www.nobelprize.org/prizes/literature/2018/tokarczuk/lecture/.
2. Steffensen, Victor. *Fire Country: How Indigenous Fire Management Could Help Save Australia*. Melbourne, Australia: Hardie Grant Pub., 2020, 145
3. Steffensen, 147.
4. Steffensen, 59.

5. Steffensen, 89.
6. Steffensen, 98.
7. This and subsequent quotes about the cool fire demonstration are from Steffensen, 90–94.
8. Steffensen, 147
9. Steffensen, 147.
10. Steffensen, 193.
11. Baldwin, James. "Nothing Personal." *Contributions in Black Studies* vol. 6, article 5, September 2008, 12.